Essential
Spanish Grammar

Essential Spanish Grammar

By
SEYMOUR RESNICK
Professor of Romance Languages
Queens College

Dover Publications, Inc., New York

Published in Canada by General Publishing Company, Ltd., 30 Lesmill Road, Don Mills, Toronto, Ontario.
Published in the United Kingdom by Messrs. Hodder and Stoughton, Limited, St. Paul's House, Warwick Square, London E. C. 4.

Essential Spanish Grammar is a new work, published by Dover Publications, Inc. for the first time in 1959.

Standard Book Number: 486-20780-3
Library of Congress Catalog Card Number: 63-4093

Manufactured in the United States of America
Dover Publications, Inc.
180 Varick Street
New York, N. Y. 10014

Table of Contents

Introduction

Essential Spanish Grammar assumes that you will be spending a limited number of hours studying Spanish grammar and that your limited objective is simple everyday communication. It is offered not as a condensed outline of all aspects of the grammar, but as a series of aids which will enable you to use more effectively and with greater versatility phrases and vocabulary that you have previously learned. It will familiarize you with the more common structure and patterns of the language and give you a selected number of the most useful rules and paradigms.

If you have studied Spanish in a conventional manner, you will probably understand everything in *Essential Spanish Grammar,* which could then serve as a refresher even though it takes a different approach from conventional grammars. You may want to glance through the book and then pay attention to those areas in which you are weak.

But if this is your first introduction to Spanish grammar, the following suggestions will be helpful.

1. Don't approach this book until you have mastered many useful phrases and expressions such as you will find in any good phrase book or the *Listen and Learn* course. Everything will be more comprehensible and usable after you have achieved some simple, working knowledge of the language. The purpose of this book is to enable you to achieve greater fluency with the phrase approach, not to teach you to construct sentences from rules and vocabulary.

2. Start at the beginning of this book and read through

it. Look up unfamiliar or confusing grammatical terms in the short glossary in the rear. Don't be concerned if sections are not immediately clear to you. On second or third reading they will make better sense. What may appear discouragingly difficult at first will become understandable as your studies progress. As you use the language and hear it spoken, many aspects of Spanish grammar will begin to form recognizable patterns. If *Essential Spanish Grammar* does nothing more than acquaint you with some of the structure and nature of this grammar, it will be helpful to you in developing your vocabulary, phrases and generally improving your comprehension.

3. Go back to this book periodically. Sections which seem difficult or of doubtful benefit to you now, may prove extremely helpful later on.

4. For the most part, *Essential Spanish Grammar* is presented in a logical order, especially for the major divisions of grammar, and you will do best if you follow its sequence in your studies. However, the author is aware that some students learn best when they study to answer their immediate questions and needs (e.g. how to form the comparative; the declension of the verb *to be*, etc.). If you prefer to work in this manner, study entire sections rather than isolated parts of sections.

5. Examples are given for every rule. You may find it helpful to memorize the examples. If you learn every example given in this supplement and its literal translation, you will have been exposed to the most basic problems of Spanish grammar and to examples for their solution.

There are many ways to express the same thought. Languages have different constructions for expressing the same idea; some simple, others difficult. An elusive verb conjugation may well be a more sophisticated way of expression and one you may ultimately wish to master; but during your first experiments in communication you can achieve your aim by using a simple form, which will still result in perfectly acceptable grammar. Try to work out easy ways for expressing complex ideas rather than translating ideas, word for word. Throughout this grammar you'll find helpful hints on how to avoid difficult constructions.

As you begin to speak Spanish, you will be your own best judge of the areas in which you need help in grammatical construction. If there's no one with whom to practice, speak mentally to yourself. In the course of a day, see how many of the simple thoughts you've expressed in English can be stated in some manner in Spanish. This kind of experimental self-testing will give direction to your study of grammar. Remember that you are studying this course in Spanish not to pass an examination or receive a certificate, but to communicate with others on a simple but useful level. *Essential Spanish Grammar* is not the equivalent of a formal course of study at a university. Although it could serve as a supplement to a formal course, its primary aim is to help the adult study on his own. Indeed, no self study or academic course could ever be offered that is ideally suited to every potential student. You must therefore rely on and be guided by your own rate of learning, your own requirements and interests.

If this grammar or any other grammar tends to inhibit your use of the language you may have learned through a simple phrase approach as taught in some schools and the *Listen and Learn* records, curtail your study of grammar until you really feel it will assist rather than hinder your speaking.   Your objective is speaking and you *can* learn to speak a language without formal grammatical training.   The fundamental purpose of *Essential Spanish Grammar* is to enable you to learn more rapidly and eliminate hit-or-miss memorization.   For those who are at home with a more systematic approach, grammar [will enable them to learn more quickly.

The primary purpose of this grammar is not to teach you perfect Spanish but to communicate and make yourself understood.   If its goal is achieved, you will be speaking Spanish and making mistakes rather than maintaining a discreet silence.   In most cases, it is better to speak and make mistakes than not to speak at all.   *Se aprende a hablar, hablando.*   One learns to speak by speaking.

Abbreviations used in *Essential Spanish Grammar*

M.	Masculine
F.	Feminine
SING.	Singular
PL.	Plural
LIT.	Literally
Ud., Vd.	Usted
Uds., Vds.	Ustedes

Italics and bold faces have been used in this grammar to make important points more obvious to you. These diversities in type do not mean that Spanish is written or printed in varying type faces. Nor do they mean that special stress or accent is given to syllables or words.   They are used purely as a typographical convenience, to make you remember endings or to call your attention to key words.

Vocabulary and Vocabulary Building

The following suggestions may be helpful to you in building your vocabulary:

1. Study words and word lists that answer real and preferably immediate personal needs. If you are planning to travel in the near future your motivation and orientation is clear cut and *Listen and Learn* or any good phrase book gives you the material you will need. Select material according to your personal interests and requirements. If you don't plan to motor, don't spend time studying parts of the car. If you like foreign foods, study the supplementary foreign food list. Even if you do not plan to travel in the near future, you will probably learn more quickly by imagining yourself in a travel or real life situation.

2. Use the mnemonic technique of association. For the most part, *Listen and Learn* or a phrase book gives you associated word lists. If you continue to build your vocabulary by memorization don't use a dictionary for this purpose. Select such grammars or books that have lists of associated words.

3. Study the specialized vocabulary of your profession, business or hobby. If you are interested in real estate learn the many terms associated with property, buying, selling, leasing etc. An interest in mathematics should lead you to a wide vocabulary in this science. Words in your specialty will be learned quickly and a surprising amount will be applicable or transferable to other areas. Although these specialized vocabularies are not readily available in book literature, an active interest and a good dictionary are all you really need.

11

Word Order

Word order in Spanish is frequently the same as in English. Since many words in Spanish are obviously related in appearance and derivation to English words, it is often a simple matter to understand a Spanish sentence if you know only a minimum of grammar.*

Madrid está en el centro de la península ibérica.	Madrid is in the center of the Iberian peninsula.
Los turistas generalmente visitan los puntos de interés.	The tourists generally visit the points of interest.

How to Turn a Positive Sentence into a Negative Sentence

You can convert any of the sentences in your phrase book or records into negative sentences by simply placing *no* (which means both *no* and *not*) before the verb of the sentence.

Esta ciudad *no* es muy grande.	This city is *not* very large
Yo *no* hablo muy bien.	I do *not* speak very well.

How to Form Questions

There are three very easy ways to turn ordinary statements into questions. You can take almost any sentence out of your phrase book, and by treating it in one of these three ways make it a question.

* If you are not clear about the terms and concepts used in grammar, we suggest that you read the glossary of grammatical terms at the end of this book before you begin your study of Spanish.

1. It is possible to form a question in Spanish without changing the original word order at all, simply by raising your voice. We sometimes do this in English, too. In written Spanish you are warned that a question is coming by an inverted question mark at the beginning of the sentence.

¿Usted habla inglés?	Do you speak English?

2. We may also form questions by placing the predicate in front of the subject of the sentence. This same construction is used in English.

¿Es importante el primer capítulo?	Is the first chapter important?
¿Habla usted inglés?	Do you speak English?

3. A third common way of making an ordinary statement into a question is by adding *¿no?* or *¿verdad?* or *¿no es verdad?* to the end of the statement. These correspond to the English phrases *Isn't it? Don't you? Aren't you? Didn't they?* etc.

Usted habla inglés, *¿verdad?*	You speak English, *don't you?*
El primer capítulo es importante, *¿no?*	The first chapter is important, *isn't it?*

Study the following sentences, which contain the most important interrogative words. For the written language, note that all these interrogative words bear a written accent.

¿*Qué* desea usted?	*What* do you wish?
¿*Cómo* puedo ir al centro?	*How* can I go downtown?
¿*Cuándo* sale el último tren?	*When* does the last train leave?
¿*Dónde* está la estación?	*Where* is the station?

¿Cuál prefiere usted?	*Which* one do you prefer?
¿Cuánto cuesta?	*How much* does it cost?
¿Cuántos necesita usted?	*How many* do you need?
¿Por qué está usted tan cansado?	*Why* are you so tired?
¿De quién es este reloj?	*Whose* watch is this?
¿Quién sabe?	*Who* knows?

Nouns

All nouns in Spanish are either masculine or feminine. Almost all nouns ending in -*o* are masculine, while those ending in -*a*, or -*d*, or -*ción* are usually feminine. (Two important exceptions are *la mano, the hand,* and *el día, the day,* which are respectively, feminine and masculine.)   With other endings you have to learn the gender when you learn the noun.   The easiest way of doing this is by learning the word *the* along with the noun.   The masculine singular form is *el*, masculine plural is *los*; feminine singular is *la*, feminine plural is *las*.

To form the plural of nouns just add -*s* to words ending with a vowel, and -*es* to words ending with a consonant.   Study the following examples:

el profesor the teacher	la mujer the woman
los profesor*es* the teachers	las mujer*es* the women
el libro the book	la camisa the shirt
los libro*s* the books	las camisa*s* the shirts
el guante the glove	la lección the lesson
los guante*s* the gloves	las leccion*es* the lessons

Many masculine nouns ending in -*o*, referring to persons, have a feminine equivalent in -*a*.

el hij*o*	the son	el amig*o* the friend (M.)	
la hij*a*	the daughter	la amig*a* the friend (F.)	
el chic*o*	the boy	el herman*o* the brother	
la chic*a*	the girl	la herman*a* the sister	

The word for *a* or *an* is *un*, masculine, and *una* feminine.

un traje	a suit	*una* playa a beach	
un edificio	a building	*una* luz a light	

Adjectives

In Spanish, adjectives have to agree in number and gender with the nouns they accompany. We have nothing comparable to this in English. In most cases, also contrary to English usage, adjectives follow their nouns.

If the masculine form of the adjective ends in -*o*, the feminine form ends in -*a*, and the plurals are -*os* and -*as* respectively.

el señor simpátic*o*	the charming gentle-man
la señora simpátic*a*	the charming lady
los señor*es* simpátic*os*	the charming gentle-men
las señor*as* simpátic*as*	the charming ladies

If the masculine singular of the adjective ends in -*e*,

the feminine singular is the same as the masculine, and the plural for both genders is formed by adding -*s*.

un país important*e*	an important country
una familia important*e*	an important family
país*es* important*es*	important countries
familias important*es*	important families

If the masculine adjectival form ends in a consonant, there is no change for the feminine singular, and we form the plural of both genders by adding -*es*.

un juego difícil	a difficult game
una lengua difícil	a difficult language
jueg*os* difícil*es*	difficult games
lengu*as* difícil*es*	difficult languages

Adverbs

In English we often form adverbs by adding -*ly* to an adjective, as in *clear, clearly, new, newly.* In Spanish many adverbs are formed similarly by adding -*mente* to the feminine form of the adjective.

absolut*o* absolute	
absoluta*mente* absolutely	
clar*o* clear	
clara*mente* clearly	
rápid*o* rapid	
rápida*mente* rapidly	

Usted debe hablar más claramente.	You ought to speak more clearly.

Two common adverbs that do not end in -*mente* are : *despacio, slowly* and *demasiado, too much.*

Expressing Possession

The English way of expressing possession by apostrophe s, *teacher's book*, is not used in Spanish. Instead, forms comparable to the other English style, *the book of the teacher*, are used.

el palacio *del* rey	the palace *of the* king (the king's palace)
las casas *de* mi padre	the houses *of* my father (my father's houses)

Note that in Spanish the definite article can often be used to indicate possession with parts of the body and articles of clothing.

Déme *la* mano.	Give me your hand.
Me quité *los* zapatos.	I took off my shoes.

The possessive adjectives are as follows:

SING.	PL.	
mi	mis	my
su	sus	your (SING.), his, her, its
nuestro (M.)	nuestros (M.)	our
nuestra (F.)	nuestras (F.)	
su	sus	your (PL.), their

Observe that these words, like other adjectives, have to agree in number and gender with the noun that they accompany.

Necesito *mi* pasaporte.	I need my passport.
¿Dónde están nuestr*as* maletas?	Where are our valises?
¿Cuál es *su* dirección?	What is your address?

After the verb *ser*, *to be*, we use special forms to express ownership.

SING.	PL.	
mío (M.),	míos	mine
mía (F.)	mías	,,
suyo (M.), suya (F.)	suyos, suyas	yours, his, her, its
nuestro (M.)	nuestros,	ours
nuestra (F.)	nuestras	,,
suyo (M.), suya (F.)	suyos, suyas	yours, theirs

These forms, too, must agree with the nouns they accompany, even though the noun is separated from them by forms of the verb, *to be*.

Este coche no es *mío*.	This car isn't mine.
Los papeles blancos son nuestros.	The white papers are ours.

Demonstrative Adjectives and Pronouns

This and *that*, *these* and *those*, are translated as follows:

este hombre	this man	*esta* mujer	this woman
estos hombres	these men	*estas* mujeres	these women
ese hombre	that man	*esa* mujer	that woman
esos hombres	those men	*esas* mujeres	those women

That may also be translated as *aquel* (M.), *aquella* (F.), *aquellos* (M.PL.), *aquellas* (F.PL.), when it refers to something in the distance.

Mire usted *aquellas* montañas.	Look at *those* mountains.

The neuter demonstrative pronouns are *esto* and *eso* for *this* and *that* respectively.

¿Qué es *esto*?	What is *this*?
Eso es.	*That* is it; *that* is right.

If you are referring to specific objects, and are differentiating between two or more things in a series, the adjectives above serve as pronouns, They then take a written accent (which does not affect pronunciation).

No quiero *éste*; déme *ése*, por favor.	I don't want *this one*; give me *that one*, please.
¿Cuáles prefiere usted, *éstos* o *aquéllos*?	Which ones do you prefer, *these* or *those*?

Comparisons

In English we make comparative forms by adding *-er* to the end of some adjectives, and by placing *more* in front of adverbs, nouns, and other adjectives. (Example: John is richer and more influential than Peter.) In Spanish you form such comparatives and superlatives by placing the word *más* (*more*) before the noun, adjective, or adverb concerned. The word *than* in such cases is translated by *que*.

Mi prima tiene *más* discos *que* nadie.	My cousin has *more* records *than* anyone.
Este paquete es *más* ligero *que* el suyo.	This package is light*er than* yours.
Son *más* inteligentes *que* sus vecinos.	They are *more* intelligent *than* their neighbors.
Repítalo *más* despacio.	Repeat it *more* slowly.

Los cubanos hablan *más* rápidamente *que* los mexicanos.	Cubans speak *more* rapidly *than* Mexicans.
Usted pronuncia *mejor que* yo.	You pronounce *better than* I.
Es la chica *más hermosa* del pueblo.	She is the *prettiest* girl in town.

Most adjectives and adverbs form their comparatives regularly, as above. A noteworthy exception, however, is *bueno*, (*good*), which has *mejor*, (*better*) as its comparative. *Mejor* is also the comparative for the adverb *bien*, (*well*).

Comparisons of equality (*as . . . as*) are translated *tan . . . como* with adjectives and adverbs, and *tanto, -a, -os, -as . . . como* with nouns.

Soy *tan* alto *como* mi hermano.	I am *as* tall *as* my brother.
Hable *tan* despacio *como* yo.	Speak *as* slowly *as* I do.
No tengo *tanto* dinero *como* ustedes.	I don't have *as* much money *as* you.
Nadie tiene *tantas* tarjetas *como* yo.	No one has *as* many cards *as* I do.

Pronouns

In Spanish, as in English, pronouns have different forms according to their use or position in a sentence.

The simplest forms, those which are used as subjects for sentences, are as follow:

yo	I	nosotros	we
usted	you (SING.)	ustedes	you (PL.)
él	he	ellos	they (M.)
ella	she	ellas	they (F.)

Direct and Indirect Object Pronouns

The object pronouns (*me, you, him, her, it, us, them*) are either direct (He takes *it*) or indirect (He gives *me* the book, or, He gives the book to *me*). In Spanish the *object* pronouns are as follows:

	Indirect		*Direct*
me	(to) me	me	me
		le	you, him
le	(to) you, him, her, it	lo	him, it (M.)
		la	you, her, it (F.)
nos	(to) us	nos	us
les	(to) you, them	los	them, you (M.)
		las	them, you (F.)

Their position is before the verb. However, with the infinitive or an affirmative command they are suffixed to the end of the verb. Study the following sentences:

Nos dieron el dinero.	They gave *us* the money.
Le expliqué el problema.	I explained the problem *to him*.
No *la* veo ahora, pero *le* hablé hace media hora.	I don't see *her* now, but I spoke to *her* half an hour ago.
Quiero escuchar*los*.	I want to listen *to them*.
Díga*me* la verdad.	Tell *me* the truth.
No *me* moleste ahora.	Don't bother *me* now.

When there are two object pronouns, the indirect object precedes the direct object.

Me lo dice.	He tells it *to me*.
Díga*me*lo.	Tell it *to me*.

If both object pronouns, however, are third person, the indirect pronoun becomes *se* instead of *le* or *les*.

Se lo dice.   He tells it *to him* (*her, you, them*).

To avoid this difficult object construction we suggest that you express yourself differently.   By using the preposition *a* (*to*) and the prepositional pronouns given in the following section, you can express the same thought much more easily.

Lo dice *a él*.	He tells it *to him*.
Lo dice *a ella*.	He tells it *to her*.
Lo dice *a usted*.	He tells it *to you*.
Lo dice *a ellos*.	He tells it *to them*.

Prepositional Forms of the Personal Pronouns

The pronoun forms used after prepositions (*for, with, against, to, among*, etc.) are the same as the subject pronouns in Spanish (*yo, usted, él, ella, nosotros, ustedes, ellos, ellas*), except for the first person singular, which is *mí*, not *yo*.   Study the following:

para *mí*	for *me*	sin *usted*	without *you*
con *él**	with *him*	a *ella*	to *her*
cerca de *nosotros*	near *us*	delante de *ustedes*	in front of *you*
entre *ellos*	among *them*	por *ellas*	by *them*

Table of Personal Pronouns

To help review the pronouns presented in the last few sections, the following table of personal pronouns will be a useful reference.   For the sake of completeness we

* Note that *with me* is *conmigo*.

include the familiar singular and familiar plural forms (in parentheses), used in addressing children, close friends and relatives, and animals. These forms should be avoided by the beginner or traveler. Use *usted* for *you* (SING.) and *ustedes* for *you* (PL.).

The last column, reflexive pronoun objects, will be taken up when you study the reflexive verb on page 44.

Subject	Preposi- tional	Indirect Object	Direct Object	Reflexive Object
yo	mí	me	me	me
(tú)	(ti)	(te)	(te)	(te)
él	él	le	le, lo	se
ella	ella	le	la	se
usted	usted	le	le, la	se
nosotros	nosotros	nos	nos	nos
(vosotros)	(vosotros)	(os)	(os)	(os)
ellos	ellos	les	los	se
ellas	ellas	les	las	se
ustedes	ustedes	les	los, las	se

Note the great similarity between the subject and prepositional forms, and the closeness of indirect, direct and reflexive objects.

Negatives

As pointed out on page 12, we can make sentences negative by placing *no* before the verb. Other important negatives are *nunca*, *never*; *nada*, *nothing*; *nadie*, *nobody*. *Nunca* may either precede the verb in place of *no*, or it may follow the verb in addition to *no*.

Nunca he estado aquí.   I've *never* been here.
No he estado aquí *nunca*.   I've *never* been here.

This combination of *no*, verb and negative pronoun or adverb is called the double negative construction. *Nada* usually takes this construction.

No veo nada.	I don't see anything ("nothing").

Nadie generally precedes the verb when it is the subject and follows the verb when it is the object.

Nadie puede hacer eso.	*Nobody* can do that.
No ví a *nadie*.	I did *not* see *anyone*.

The Contractions "al" and "del"

There are only two contractions in the Spanish language. *A* and *el* become *al*, and *de* and *el* become *del*.

Mandé un telegrama *al* presidente *del* país.	I sent a telegram *to the* president *of the* country.
Vamos *al* mercado *del* pueblo.	Let's go *to the* town market.

Personal "a"

A peculiarity of Spanish is that the preposition *a* is placed before a direct object, if the object is a definite person.

¿Ha visto Vd. *a* mi primo?	Have you seen my cousin?
Busco *al* gerente.	I am looking for the manager.
Vamos a visitar *a* los señores García.	Let's visit Mr. and Mrs. García.

The Word "que"

In English we frequently omit the word *that* when it is a conjunction. (*I think that he will come*, or *I think he will come*.) In Spanish the conjunction *que* must be expressed.

Creo *que* vendrá.	I think (*that*) he will come.
¿Sabe Vd. *que* no están casados?	Do you know (*that*) they are not married?

In addition to being a conjunction, *que* is also the most important relative pronoun (*who, which, that, whom*), since it may refer to either persons or things, and may be used as either subject or object. The following sentences illustrate its uses:

No encuentro el diccionario *que* compré ayer.	I don't find the dictionary (*which*) I bought yesterday.
El hombre *que* hizo eso ya no vive aquí.	The man *who* did that no longer lives here.
Aquí tiene usted un abrigo *que* no cuesta mucho.	Here is a coat *that* does not cost much.
Es el mismo mesero *que* tuvimos ayer.	He's the same waiter (*that*) we had yesterday.

Verbs

The Present Tense

In English, verbs are rather simple. Very few endings are added, and these are relatively uniform (I sing, he sing*s*, I take, he take*s*).   In Spanish more endings are used, and these tell you the person and number of the subject.   There are three such sets of endings or conjugations; and each verb belongs to one.   You can tell the conjugation of a verb by looking at its infinitive (the form which corresponds to the English *to walk*, *to have*, etc.).   Memorize the following tables.

First conjugation   Infinitive ending *-ar*

hablar (to speak)

(yo) habl*o*	I speak, am speaking
(usted) habl*a*	you (SING.) speak, are speaking
(él, ella) habl*a*	he, she, it speaks, is speaking
(nosotros) habl*amos*	we speak, are speaking
(ustedes) habl*an*	you (PL.) speak, are speaking
(ellos, ellas) habl*an*	they speak, are speaking

Second conjugation   Infinitive ending *-er*

comer (to eat)

(yo) com*o*	I eat, am eating
(usted) com*e*	you (SING.) eat, are eating
(él, ella) com*e*	he, she, it eats, is eating
(nosotros) com*emos*	we eat, are eating
(ustedes) com*en*	you (PL.) eat, are eating
(ellos, ellas) com*en*	they eat, are eating

Third conjugation   Infinitive ending *-ir*

escribir (to write)

(yo) escrib*o*	I write, am writing
(usted) escrib*e*	you (SING.) write, are writing
(él, ella) escrib*e*	he, she, it writes, is writing
(nosotros) escrib*imos*	we write, are writing
(ustedes) escrib*en*	you (PL.) write, are writing
(ellos, ellas) escrib*en*	they write, are writing

Several points should be noted:

1. The subject pronouns *yo, él, ella, nosotros, ellos, ellas,* are often omitted. The subject pronouns *usted* and *ustedes, you,* however, are usually used.

2. The first person singular ending for all verbs (except for a few irregular instances to be given later) is *-o.*

3. The *usted* (abbreviated *Ud.* or *Vd.*) form of the verb is the same as the *él* or *ella* form, and the *ustedes* (abbreviated *Uds.* or *Vds.*) form is the same as the *ellos* or *ellas* form. In the following verb tables, therefore, only four forms will be given, instead of six.

4. The third person plural forms (*they . . .*) are formed by adding *-n* to the third person singular forms (*he . . .*), *habla, hablan; come, comen.*

5. The second and third conjugation endings are the same except for the first person plural, *-emos, -imos,* respectively.

6. The first person plural ending always has the characteristic vowel of the infinitive *-amos, -emos, -imos.*

7. The same form in Spanish can be translated as both simple present in English (*I speak*) and the progressive present (*I am speaking*).

8. Besides *usted* and *ustedes* there is another way of saying *you* in Spanish. A familiar singular form *tú* is used to address close friends, relatives, children and animals. Its verb forms end in -*s* (*hablas, you speak, comes, you eat,* and *escribes, you write*). The plural familiar form is *vosotros*, and its verb forms are *habláis, you speak, coméis, you eat,* and *escribís, you write*. You will probably have no opportunity to use these forms, and should avoid them; we mention them only so that you will recognize them if you hear them. Concentrate instead on the polite forms *usted* and *ustedes*.

Irregular Verbs

There are a few irregular verbs which are very frequently used, and which must be learned. Here is the present tense of the most important of these verbs. To simplify learning, verb conjugations are presented in the following pattern: the first person singular, second and third person singular; the first person plural, second and third person plural.

Example:

decir (to say)

digo	I say
dice	you (SING.) say; he says, she says
decimos	we say
dicen	you (PL.) say; they say

decir	to say, tell	digo, dice, decimos, dicen
hacer	to do, make	hago, hace, hacemos, hacen

oír to hear	oigo, oye, oímos, oyen
poner to put, place	pongo, pone, ponemos, ponen
salir to leave, go out	salgo, sale, salimos, salen
tener to have	tengo, tiene, tenemos, tienen
traer to bring	traigo, trae, traemos, traen
venir to come	vengo, viene, venimos, vienen
dar to give	doy, da, damos, dan
ir to go	voy, va, vamos, van
saber to know	sé, sabe, sabemos, saben
ver to see	veo, ve, vemos, ven

Stem-changing Verbs

Some verbs change their stems in the present tense of all persons except the first plural.   After dropping the infinitive ending -ar, -er, -ir, the e of the last syllable changes to ie, and an o in the last syllable changes to ue. These changes affect all three conjugations.   Some verbs of the third conjugation only, -ir, may have a change of e to i.   Study the following examples.

pensar (ie) to think	pienso, piensa, pensamos, piensan
querer (ie) to want, like, love	quiero, quiere, queremos, quieren
contar (ue) to count	cuento, cuenta, contamos, cuentan
poder (ue) to be able	puedo, puede, podemos, pueden
pedir (i) to ask (for)	pido, pide, pedimos, piden

Other common verbs of this type are given here. The change is indicated in parentheses.

cerrar (ie) to close	cierro, cierra, cerramos, cierran
comenzar (ie) to begin	comienzo, comienza, comenzamos, comienzan
costar (ue) to cost	cuesto, cuesta, costamos, cuestan
despertar (ie) to awaken	despierto, despierta, despertamos, despiertan
dormir (ue) to sleep	duermo, duerme, dormimos, duermen
empezar (ie) to begin	empiezo, empieza, empezamos, empiezan
encontrar (ue) to find, meet	encuentro, encuentra, encontramos, encuentran
entender (ie) to understand	entiendo, entiende, entendemos, entienden
jugar (ue) to play	juego, juega, jugamos, juegan
morir (ue) to die	muero, muere, morimos, mueren
mostrar (ue) to show	muestro, muestra, mostramos, muestran
perder (ie) to lose	pierdo, pierde, perdemos, pierden

preferir (ie)	to prefer	prefiero, prefiere, preferimos, prefieren
repetir (i)	to repeat	repito, repite, repetimos, repiten
seguir (i)	to follow	sigo, sigue, seguimos, siguen
sentar (ie)	to seat	siento, sienta, sentamos, sientan
sentir (ie)	to regret, feel	siento, siente, sentimos, sienten
servir (i)	to serve	sirvo, sirve, servimos, sirven
vestir (i)	to dress	visto, viste, vestimos, visten
volar (ue)	to fly	vuelo, vuela, volamos, vuelan
volver (ue),	to return	vuelvo, vuelve, volvemos, vuelven

The Verbs "Ser" and "Estar"

In English, although we do not realize it when we speak, we express many different ideas with the verb *to be*. *Are*, for example, can mean *are located* (*Granada and Barcelona are in Spain.*), *equal* (*Two and two are four.*), or *have the characteristic of being* (*Apples are red.*). Spanish, however, uses two different verbs (*estar* and *ser*) for the ideas we express with *to be*. *Estar* is used to express location and condition; condition includes adjectives that describe a state of emotion or health (*triste, sad; contento, glad; enfermo, sick; cansado, tired,* etc.). *Ser* is used in most other cases, especially to indicate a permanent quality. Memorize the irregular present

tense of these important verbs and study the following
sentences.

estar	ser	to be
estoy	soy	I am
está	es	you are (SING.); he, she, it is
estamos	somos	we are
están	son	you are (PL.), they are

The following sentences illustrate condition or location. *Estar* is used.

Madrid está en el centro geográfico de la península ibérica.	Madrid is in the geographic center of the Iberian peninsula. (location)
La catedral no está lejos de aquí.	The cathedral is not far from here. (location)
¿Dónde están mis anteojos?	Where are my eyeglasses? (location)
¿Cómo están ustedes?	How are you? (condition)
Estamos un poquito cansados.	We are a little tired. (condition)
¿Por qué está usted tan triste hoy?	Why are you so sad today? (condition)

The following sentences are not statements of condition or location, but of essence, and *ser* is therefore used.

Somos turistas de los Estados Unidos.	We are tourists from the United States.
Madrid es la capital de España.	Madrid is the capital of Spain.

Nuestro guía es muy bueno.	Our guide is very good.
Su novia no es rica, pero es muy bella.	His girl friend is not rich, but she is very beautiful.
¿Quién es usted? Soy el señor Miller.	Who are you? I am Mr. Miller.

Estar is also used to form the progressive tense, which corresponds to the English *to be* plus a present participle (*I am walking, you are reading*, etc.). In Spanish the present participle is formed by dropping the infinitive ending *-ar, -er, -ir*, and adding *-ando* to the first conjugation, and *-iendo* to the second and third conjugations.

comprar	comprando	buying
llover	lloviendo	raining
sufrir	sufriendo	suffering

The progressive tense is more vivid than the simple present, but the simple present can always be used in Spanish.

Estoy escribiendo una carta a mi familia *or, Escribo* una carta a mi familia.	*I am writing* a letter to my family.
Estamos visitando muchos lugares hermosos *or, Visitamos* muchos lugares hermosos.	*We are visiting* many beautiful places.
¿Qué *está* usted *haciendo*? *or,* ¿Qué *hace* usted?	What *are* you *doing*?

The Command Form

To obtain the command form of almost any verb we take the first person singular of the present tense, drop the *-o*, and add the following endings: *-ar* verbs add *-e* (SING.), and *-en* (PL.), while *-er* and *-ir* verbs add *-a* (SING.) and *-an* (PL.).   For example, *to come*, is *venir*, *I come* is *vengo* (see page 29); therefore the command *Come!* is *¡Venga (Vd.)!* in the singular and *¡Vengan (Vds.)!* in the plural.   Notice that the pronoun, when it is used, is placed after the verb.

bajar	to come down	baje (Vd.), bajen (Vds.)
pagar	to pay	pague (Vd.), paguen* (Vds.)
recordar	to remember	recuerde (Vd.), recuerden (Vds.)
comer	to eat	coma (Vd.), coman (Vds.)
escribir	to write	escriba (Vd.), escriban (Vds.)
servir	to serve	sirva (Vd.), sirvan (Vds.)
volver	to return	vuelva (Vd.), vuelvan (Vds.)
decir	to say, tell	diga (Vd.), digan (Vds.)

The command is usually softened and rendered more polite by adding *por favor*, *please*.

Abra Vd. la ventana, por favor.	Please open the window.
Siéntese, por favor.	Please sit down.
Tráigame otro vaso, por favor.	Please bring me another glass.

* Since *g* before *e* or *i* has the sound of a harsh *h*, *u* must be inserted in these forms to keep the hard *g* sound of the infinitive.

Another way of expressing a command is to use the phrase *Hágame Vd. el favor de* with the infinitive, *Do me the favor of* . . .

Hágame Vd. el favor de abrir la ventana.	Please open the window.
Hágame Vd. el favor de traducir esta frase.	Please translate this sentence.

The verb *ir, to go,* has an irregular command: *vaya Vd.* and *vayan Vds.*

Vaya con Dios.	Go with God.*

The first person plural command form (*let's,* with the infinitive) is best translated by *vamos a* with the infinitive. *Vamos* alone means *let us go.*

Vamos al cine esta noche.	Let's go to the movies tonight.
Vamos a ver.	Let's see.
Vamos a cantar.	Let's sing.
Vamos a jugar.	Let's play.

The Past Tense

Spanish, like English, has several ways of expressing a past event. The past tense which will be most useful is the preterit, which corresponds to the English simple past (*I went, I left, I bought,* etc.). It is formed by dropping the infinitive ending and adding *-é, -ó, -amos, -aron* to the stem of the first conjugation, and *-í, -ió, -imos, -ieron* to the stems of the second and third conjugations.

* Often used as a way of saying *good-bye.*

First conjugation   -*ar*

comprar (to buy)

compr*é*	I bought
compr*ó*	you (SING.), he, she, it bought
compr*amos*	we bought
compr*aron*	you (PL.), they bought

Second conjugation   -*er*

perder (to lose)

perd*í*	I lost
perd*ió*	you, he, she, it lost
perd*imos*	we lost
perd*ieron*	you, they lost

Third conjugation   -*ir*

salir (to leave)

sal*í*	I left
sal*ió*	you, he, she, it left
sal*imos*	we left
sal*ieron*	you, they left

There are some important verbs which are irregular in the preterit. These should be memorized.

dar	to give	dí, dió, dimos, dieron
decir	to say, tell	dije, dijo, dijimos, dijeron
estar	to be	estuve, estuvo, estuvimos, estuvieron
hacer	to do, make	hice, hizo, hicimos, hicieron
ir	to go	fuí, fué, fuimos, fueron
ser	to be	fuí, fué, fuimos, fueron
poner	to put, place	puse, puso, pusimos, pusieron
tener	to have	tuve, tuvo, tuvimos, tuvieron

traer to bring	traje, trajo, trajimos, trajeron
venir to come	vine, vino, vinimos, vinieron

Observe that the verbs *ir* and *ser* have the same preterit forms.

Study the following sentences.

Llegaron ayer y *fueron* inmediatamente al consulado americano.	*They arrived* yesterday and *went* to the American consulate immediately.
¿Qué *hizo* usted anoche?	What *did* you *do* last night?
Llamé a Juan y *fuimos* juntos al teatro.	*I called* John and *we went* to the theatre together.

The Imperfect Tense

The imperfect tense describes what was happening or what used to happen. It is formed by dropping the infinitive ending and adding -*aba*, -*aba*, -*ábamos*, -*aban* to the stem of first conjugation verbs, and -*ía*, -*ía*, -*íamos*, -*ían* to the stems of second and third conjugation verbs.

First conjugation   -*ar*

pagar (to pay)

pag*aba*	I paid, used to pay, was paying
pag*aba*	you, he, she, it paid, used to pay, was paying, were paying
pag*ábamos*	we paid, used to pay, were paying
pag*aban*	you, they, paid, used to pay, were paying

Second conjugation   -er

creer (to believe)

creía	I believed, used to believe
creía	you, he, she, it believed, used to believe
creíamos	we believed, used to believe
creían	they, you believed, used to believe

Third conjugation   -ir

vivir (to live)

vivía	I lived, used to live, was living
vivía	you, he, she, it lived, used to live, was living, were living
vivíamos	we lived, used to live, were living
vivían	you, they lived, used to live, were living

There are only three verbs with irregular imperfects.

ir to go	iba, iba, íbamos, iban
ser to be	era, era, éramos, eran
ver to see	veía, veía, veíamos, veían

Observe that in all verbs the first, second and third person singular imperfect are identical.

The following sentences will help to show the difference in use between the imperfect and the preterit.

Le *veía* todos los días.	*I used to see* him every day.
Le *vi* ayer.	*I saw* him yesterday.
¿Qué *hacía* usted cuando llamé?	What *were* you *doing* when I called?
¿Qué *hizo* usted cuando llamé?	What *did* you *do* when I called?
Cuando *éramos* chicos *íbamos* al cine todos los sábados.	When *we were* kids, *we used to go* to the movies every Saturday.

The preterit will be far more useful to you than the imperfect. The imperfect of the following verbs, however, is used more frequently than the preterit:

quería	I wanted	esperaba	I hoped
creía	I believed	tenía	I had
podía	I could	sabía	I knew

Creía que no *teníamos* el dinero.	*He thought we didn't have* the money.
Quería verla.	*I wanted* to see her.
No *sabía* si *iban* a venir, pero lo *esperaba*.	*I didn't know* if *they were going* to come, but *I hoped* so.

The Present Perfect and Pluperfect

Just like English, Spanish has two compound past tenses, the present perfect (*I have spoken, I have seen*, etc.) and the pluperfect (*I had spoken, I had seen*, etc.). They are formed and used almost exactly as in English. The Spanish equivalent of the English auxiliary verb *have* is *haber*. Its present tense is

haber to have (auxiliary)*	he, ha, hemos, han

The present perfect is formed by taking the present of *haber* and the past participle of a verb (formed by dropping the infinitive ending and adding -*ado* to the first conjugation and -*ido* to the second and third).

In English the word *have* is also used to indicate possession. In Spanish *haber* is never used in this sense. *Tener* is used to indicate possession.

First conjugation

visitar (to visit)

he visitado	I have visited
ha visitado	you have visited, he, she, it has visited
hemos visitado	we have visited
han visitado	you, they have visited

Second conjugation

escoger (to choose)

he escogido	I have chosen
ha escogido	you have chosen, he, she, it has chosen
hemos escogido	we have chosen
han escogido	you, they have chosen

Third conjugation

insistir (to insist)

he insistido	I have insisted
ha insistido	you have insisted, he, she, it has insisted
hemos insistido	we have insisted
han insistido	you, they have insisted

The pluperfect tense is formed with the imperfect of *haber* (*había, había, habíamos, habían*) and the past participle.

gastar (to spend)

había gastado	I had spent
había gastado	you, he, she, it had spent
habíamos gastado	we had spent
habían gastado	they, you had spent

¿Han visitado Uds. el museo?	Have you visited the museum?

Hemos gastado mucho dinero.	We have spent a lot of money.
Nunca había vivido en un país extranjero.	I had never lived in a foreign country.

The following verbs have irregular past participles: abrir, abierto (opened); escribir, escrito (written); morir, muerto (died); poner, puesto (put); ver, visto (seen); volver, vuelto (returned); decir, dicho (said); hacer, hecho (done).

¿Qué *ha dicho* Ud.?	What *have* you *said*?
Ya *había muerto.*	He *had* already *died.*
¿Dónde *ha puesto* Ud. la llave?	Where *have* you *put* the key?

Remember that the preterit or simple past is the past tense you should use most of the time. If you lack the time to learn the other past tenses, you can get along without them.

The Future Tense

The future tense is formed by adding -*é*, -*á*, -*emos*, -*án* to the entire infinitive for all three conjugations.

First conjugation

explicar (to explain)

explicar*é*	I shall explain
explicar*á*	you (SING.), he, she, it will explain
explicar*emos*	we shall explain
explicar*án*	you (PL.), they will explain

Second conjugation

ver (to see)

ver*é*	I shall see
ver*á*	you, he, she, it will see
ver*emos*	we shall see
ver*án*	you, they will see

Third conjugation

abrir (to open)

abrir*é*	I shall open
abrir*á*	you, he, she, it will open
abrir*emos*	we shall open
abrir*án*	they will open

The following common verbs have irregular stems in the future.

decir	to say, tell	diré, dirá, diremos, dirán
hacer	to do, make	haré, hará, haremos, harán
poder	to be able	podré, podrá, podremos, podrán
poner	to put, place	pondré, pondrá, pondremos, podrán
saber	to know	sabré, sabrá, sabremos, sabrán
salir	to leave	saldré, saldrá, saldremos, saldrán
tener	to have (possession)	tendré, tendrá, tendremos, tendrán
venir	to come	vendré, vendrá, vendremos, vendrán

Study the following sentences illustrating the use of the future which corresponds to English.

¿Qué *harán* ustedes mañana?	What *will* you *do* tomorrow?
No sé, pero creo que *podremos* visitar a algunos amigos.	I don't know but I think that *we'll be able* to visit some friends.

Volveremos temprano porque *iremos* al teatro después.	*We'll* return early because *we'll* go to the theatre later.
¿Cuándo *saldrá usted* para Guadalajara? Mañana si consigo boleto en el avión de la tarde; si no, *tendré* que tomar el autobús y no *llegaré* hasta el lunes.	When *will you leave* for Guadalajara? Tomorrow, if I get a ticket on the afternoon plane; if not, *I shall have* to take the bus and *shall* not *arrive* until Monday.

In English we frequently express the idea of futurity by using the verb *to go* with an infinitive. Similarly in Spanish we may use *ir a* with an infinitive.

¿Qué *van* ustedes *a* hacer?	What *are* you *going* to do?
Vamos a volver temprano porque *vamos a* ir al teatro después.	*We're going* to come back early because *we're going* to go to the theater later.

Both in English and in Spanish we sometimes use the present tense instead of the future. For the beginner, this can be a useful alternate.

¿Qué *hacen Vds.* mañana?	What *are you doing* tomorrow?
¿Cuándo *sale Vd.* para Cuba?	When *are you leaving* for Cuba?

The Conditional

The conditional and past conditional are used as in English. To form the conditional add the endings

-ía, -ía, -íamos, -ían to the infinitive for all three conjugations.

ir (to go)

iría	I would go
iría	you, he, she, it would go
iríamos	we would go
irían	you, they would go

Verbs that have an irregular stem in the future have the same stem for the conditional:

diría	I would say, tell
haría	I would do, make
podría	I would be able
pondría	I would put
sabría	I would know
saldría	I would leave
tendría	I would have (possession)
vendría	I would come

To form the past conditional (*would have* and past participle in English) we take the conditional of *haber* and the past participle.

habría volado	I would have flown
habría volado	you, he, she, it would have flown
habríamos volado	we would have flown
habrían volado	you, they would have flown

Reflexive Verbs

In English we say *I got up at seven, I washed, shaved, and dressed.* In Spanish, however, each of these verbs (*got up, washed, shaved, dressed*) must be used with a special reflexive pronoun; they are called reflexive verbs.

Me levanté a las siete, me lavé, me afeité, y me vestí.	· (*Lit.*) I got myself up at seven, I washed myself, I shaved myself, and I dressed myself.

Reflexive verbs are indicated in the dictionary by -*se* added to the infinitive: *levantarse, lavarse, vestirse.*

You need learn only three reflexive pronouns:

me	myself
se	yourself, himself, herself, itself, yourselves, themselves
nos	ourselves

These pronouns are placed in front of the verb, in all forms except the infinitive and affirmative command, where they are placed directly on the end of the verb. We shall use the verb *sentarse, to sit down,* to illustrate the conjugation of a reflexive verb.

Present

me siento	I sit down
se sienta	you sit down, he, she, it sits down
nos sentamos	we sit down
se sientan	you, they sit down

Past

me senté	I sat down
se sentó	you, he, she, it sat down
nos sentamos	we sat down
se sentaron	you, they sat down

Future

me sentaré	I shall sit down
se sentará	you, he, she, it will sit down
nos sentaremos	we shall sit down
se sentarán	you, they will sit down

Commands

¡siénte*se* [Vd.]!	Sit down. (to one person)
¡siénten*se* [Vds.]!	Sit down. (to more than one person)
¡no *se* siente [Vd.]!	Don't sit down. (to one person)
¡no *se* sienten [Vds.]!	Don't sit down. (to more than one person)

Here is a list of the most important reflexive verbs. The *ie, ue,* or *i* in parentheses indicates that the stem of the verb changes in the present.

acostarse (ue) to go to bed	afeitarse to shave
alegrarse to be glad	casarse to get married
despedirse (i) to say goodby	despertarse (ie) to wake up
divertirse (ie) to have a good time	lavarse to wash (oneself)
levantarse to get up	llamarse to be called
ponerse to put on	quejarse to complain
sentarse (ie) to sit down	quitarse to take off
vestirse (i) to get dressed	sentirse (ie) to feel

Study the following examples which illustrate verbs used in nonreflexive and reflexive forms:

El barbero no me afeitó bien.	The barber didn't shave me well.
Me afeito todos los días.	I shave (myself) every day.
Llamé a mi amigo.	I called my friend.
¿Cómo *se* llama usted?	What is your name? (*Lit.* How do you call yourself?)
Me llamo Miguel Gómez.	My name is Michael Gómez (*Lit.* I call myself Michael Gómez.)
Lavo los platos después de la comida.	I wash the dishes after dinner.
Me lavo las manos antes de comer.	I wash my hands before eating.

Other Examples of the Reflexive

In Spanish the reflexive is often used to express the English indefinite (*one, you, they* . . .) constructions and the passive (*to be* with a past participle). Note that the subject usually follows the verb in this construction.

Se habla portugués en el Brasil.	(*Lit.* Portuguese speaks itself in Brazil.) They speak Portuguese in Brazil. Portuguese is spoken in Brazil. One speaks Portuguese in Brazil.

¿Cómo *se* dice esto en español?	(*Lit.* How does this say itself in Spanish?)
	How do you say this in Spanish?
	How is this said in Spanish?
	How does one say this in Spanish?
¿Cómo *se* puede ir de aquí al centro?	(*Lit.* How is it possible to go from here to the main part of the town?)
	How can one (I, you, we) go from here to the main part of the town?
Se prohibe fumar.	No smoking. Smoking is prohibited.
Se venden sombreros en esta tienda.	Hats are sold in this store.
El banco *se* cierra a las tres.	The bank closes (is closed) at three.

If, however, the person doing the action is expressed, we must use the true passive construction, which is the same as in English—the verb *to be* with a past participle. Note that the verb *to be* is translated by *ser* and that the past participle agrees with the subject in gender and number. Study the following examples:

Las cartas *fueron escritas* por la secretaria.	The letters *were written* by the secretary.
Este edificio *fué construido* por mi compañía.	This building *was constructed* by my company.

The Subjunctive

The subjunctive is very little used in English, but is quite frequent and important in Spanish. We are presenting briefly its formation and main uses, primarily for recognition when you see it or hear it, although correct use of the subjunctive in conversation is not difficult.

Formation of the Subjunctive Tenses; Present Subjunctive

We first came upon the subjunctive, without knowing it, when we learned the command form (p. 34), which is really part of the subjunctive. The present subjunctive of almost all verbs is formed by taking the first person singular (the *yo* form) of the present indicative (pp. 25–27), dropping the -*o*, and adding, for -*ar* verbs, -*e*, -*e*, -*emos*, -*en*; for -*er* and -*ir* verbs, -*a*, -*a*, -*amos*, -*an*:

INFINITIVE		1ST PERS. SING.	PRES. SUBJUNCTIVE
hablar	to speak	habl*o*	habl*e*, habl*e*, habl*emos*, habl*en*
comer	to eat	com*o*	com*a*, com*a*, com*amos*, com*an*
escribir	to write	escrib*o*	escríb*a*, escrib*a*, escrib*amos*, escrib*an*

Note the spelling changes necessary in verbs ending in -*car* and -*gar*:

INFINITIVE		1ST PERS. SING.	PRES. SUBJUNCTIVE
buscar	to seek	busc*o*	busque, busque, busquemos, busquen
pagar	to pay	pag*o*	pague, pague, paguemos, paguen

As with commands, verbs that are irregular in the first person singular of the present indicative (pp. 28–29) are irregular in the subjunctive. The following are the most important:

INFINITIVE		IST PERS. SING.	PRES. SUBJUNCTIVE
decir	to say, tell	digo	diga, diga, digamos, digan
hacer	to do, make	hago	haga, haga, hagamos, hagan
oír	to hear	oigo	oiga, oiga, oigamos, oigan
poner	to put, place	pongo	ponga, ponga, pongamos, pongan
salir	to leave, go out	salgo	salga, salga, salgamos, salgan
tener	to have	tengo	tenga, tenga, tengamos, tengan
venir	to come	vengo	venga, venga, vengamos, vengan
ver	to see	veo	vea, vea, veamos, vean

Note the following irregular subjunctives not formed on the stem of the first person singular of the present indicative:

dar	to give	dé, dé, demos, den
estar	to be	esté, esté, estemos, estén
haber	to have (auxiliary)	haya, haya, hayamos, hayan
ir	to go	vaya, vaya, vayamos, vayan
saber	to know	sepa, sepa, sepamos, sepan
ser	to be	sea, sea, seamos, sean

The other tenses of the subjunctive are formed as follows:

Present Perfect Subjunctive

The present perfect subjunctive in Spanish is formed with the present subjunctive of the auxiliary verb *haber* and the past participle of the main verb:

hacer	to do, make	haya (haya, hayamos, hayan) hecho
ver	to see	haya (haya, hayamos, hayan) visto

Imperfect Subjunctive

The imperfect subjunctive is formed by dropping the *-ron* of the third person plural (the *ellos* form) of the preterit tense (pp. 35–37), and adding *-ra, -ra, -'ramos, -ran* or *-se, -se, -'semos, -sen*:

INF.	3RD PERS. PL. PRETERIT	IMPERFECT SUBJUNCTIVE
hacer	hicieron	hicie*ra*, hicie*ra*, hicié*ramos*, hicie*ran*
	OR	hicie*se*, hicie*se*, hicié*semos*, hicie*sen*

Pluperfect Subjunctive

The pluperfect subjunctive is formed by placing the imperfect subjunctive of the auxiliary verb *haber* before the past participle of the main verb:

tomar	to take	hubiera, hubiera, hubiéramos, hubieran hubiese, hubiese, hubiésemos, hubiesen } tomado

Generally, if the verb in the main clause is in the present, future or command form, the subjunctive verb will be in the present or present perfect; if the main verb is in the past, the subjunctive will be imperfect or pluperfect. The model sentences in the following section will illustrate the uses of the tenses, as well as possible translations of the subjunctive.

Uses of the Subjunctive

The main uses of the subjunctive are as follows:

1. After the verb *querer* (to want) when there is a change of subject in the subordinate clause:

Quiero que Vd. lo *haga*.	I want you to *do* it. (*Lit.* I want that you *do* it.)
Quería que Vd. lo *hiciera*.	I wanted you to *do* it.

But use the infinitive as in English if there is no change of subject:

Quiero *hacer*lo.	I want *to do* it.

2. When one person *tells* (*decir*) or *asks* (*pedir*) another person to do something:

Dígale que lo *escriba*.	Tell him to *write* it.
Me dijo que lo *escribiera*.	He told me to *write* it.
Nos piden que *salgamos*.	They are asking us to *leave*.

3. After expressions of emotion, such as *esperar* (to hope), *sentir* (to be sorry), *temer* (to fear), *alegrarse* (to be glad), when there is a change of subject:

Espero que *vuelvan*.	I hope *they return*.
Espero que *hayan vuelto*.	I hope *they have returned*.

Sentía que *vinieran*.	I was sorry *they were coming*.
Sentía que *hubieran venido*.	I was sorry *they had come*.
BUT: Me alegro de *estar* aquí.	I am glad *to be* here.

4. After *dudar* (to doubt) and other verbs expressing uncertainty:

Dudo que lo *hagan*.	I doubt that *they are doing it* (*they will do it*).
Dudo que lo *hayan hecho*.	I doubt that *they have done it*.
Dudaba que lo *hicieran*.	I doubted that *they were doing it* (*they would do it*).
Dudaba que lo *hubieran hecho*.	I doubted that *they had done it*.

5. After most impersonal expressions, such as *es posible* (it is possible), *es importante* (it is important), *es necesario*, *es preciso* (it is necessary), *es natural* (it is natural), if there is a subject for the subordinate verb:

Es posible que *vayan*.	It is possible that *they will go*.
Era preciso que *fueran*.	It was necessary for them to *go*.
Es natural que Vd. *diga* eso.	It is natural for you to *say* that.
BUT: Es imposible *hacerlo*.	It is impossible *to do* it.

6. In adjective clauses if the antecedent is indefinite:

Busco a alguien que *hable* inglés.	I am looking for someone who *speaks* English.

7. After certain adverbial conjunctions, such as *para que* (in order that), *sin que* (without), *antes que* (before):

Lo repite para que todos *entiendan*.	He is repeating it so that everyone *may understand*.
Salió sin que nadie le *viera*.	He left without anyone's *seeing* him.
Lo haré antes que *vuelvan*.	I shall do it before *they return*.

8. After time conjunctions, such as *cuando* (when), *en cuanto* (as soon as), *hasta que* (until), when futurity is implied:

Cuando le *vea*, se lo diré.	When *I see* him, I shall tell it to him.
BUT: Cuando le *vi*, se lo dije.	When *I saw* him, I told it to him.

9. In contrary-to-fact conditions, the imperfect or pluperfect subjunctive must be used in the if-clause, with the conditional or past conditional, respectively, in the main clause:

Si *tuviera* el dinero, lo compraría.	If *I had* the money, I would buy it.
Si *hubiera tenido* el dinero, lo habría comprado.	If *I had had* the money, I would have bought it.

10. The *-ra* imperfect subjunctive forms of three verbs are often used with a conditional value in a main clause:

querer – quisiera   I would like
deber – debiera   I should, I ought to
poder – pudiera   I could, would be able to

Quisiéramos ir con Vd.   We *would like* to go with you.

Vds. *debieran* visitarlo.   You *ought* to visit it.
¿*Pudiera* Vd. ayudarme?   *Could* you help me?

Special Constructions with Verbs

English and Spanish have many parallel constructions, but each one also has many idiomatic constructions which cannot be translated literally from one language to the other. In the next few pages we shall call attention to the most useful of these special expressions.

The Verb "Gustar"

The English verb *to like* is usually translated by the Spanish verb *gustar, to please*. The sentence, *I like this city*, must be changed mentally to, *This city pleases me*, before putting it into Spanish. The subject generally comes at the end of the sentence in this construction.

Me gusta esta ciudad.	I like this city. (*Lit.* This city pleases me.)
No me gusta.	I don't like it. (*Lit.* It does not please me.)
Le gustan mucho.	He likes them very much.
Nos gusta viajar.	We like to travel.
Me gustaría ir a Sevilla.	I would like to go to Seville.

When eating in someone's presence, you must offer some of your food by saying *¿Gusta?, Will you have some?* Courtesy demands that the offer be declined by saying *Gracias, que le aproveche, Thank you, good appetite*.

The Verb "Hacer"

In addition to being one of the common verbs in the language, *hacer, to do, make* is also used in a variety of

idiomatic constructions.   Here are the most useful of
these expressions.

1. Expressions of weather.

¿Qué tiempo hace?	How is the weather?
Hace buen (mal) tiempo.	The weather is fine (bad).
Hace frío.	It's cold.
Hace mucho calor.	It's very warm.
No hace mucho sol.	It's not very sunny.
But:	
Está lloviendo.	It's raining.
Está nevando.	It's snowing.

2. To translate the English *ago* we use the third person
singular of *hacer* and the length of time.

Llegué hace tres días.	I arrived three days ago.

3. Action continued from the past to the present.   To
express an action that began in the past and still con-
tinues, we use the following formula: *Hace + time + que + verb in present tense.*

Hace mucho tiempo que viven aquí.	They have been living here for a long time. (*Lit.* It makes much time that they live here.)
Hace más de dos horas que espero.	I've been waiting more than two hours. (*Lit.* It makes more than two hours that I wait.)

The ordinary present perfect tense may be used as

in English to express these ideas instead of the *hace* construction.

Han vivido aquí mucho tiempo.	They've lived here a long time.
He esperado más de dos horas.	I've waited more than two hours.

4. Note also the following idiomatic uses of *hacer*:

Hacer un viaje.	To take a trip.
Hacer una maleta.	To pack a suitcase.
Se hace tarde.	It's getting late.
No le hace.	It makes no difference.
No haga caso.	Don't pay attention to it.
Se hizo rico.	He became rich.
Se hizo daño al caer.	He hurt himself on falling.
Si me hace el favor.	Please.

Hay and Había

Hay translates *there is* and *there are*; *había* translates *there was* and *there were*.

Hay muchas turistas este año.	*There are* many tourists this year.
Había tantas cosas que ver.	*There were* so many things to see.

Hay que with the infinitive translates *it is necessary, one must.*

Hay que levantarse temprano mañana.	*It is necessary* to get up early tomorrow. *We must* get up early tomorrow.

Hay que dejar la cámara con el empleado.	*One has* to leave the camera with the employee.

Es necesario with the infinitive has the same meaning, however, and is easier to use.

Es necesario pasar por la aduana en la frontera.	*It is necessary* to go through customs at the border.

The Verb "Tener"

To be hungry, thirsty, warm, etc. are rendered in Spanish by *to have hunger, thirst, warmth,* etc. The verb *tener, to have* is used in these expressions.

Tengo (mucha) hambre.	I am (very) hungry.
Tengo (mucha) sed.	I am (very) thirsty.
Tengo (mucho) calor.	I am (very) warm.
Tengo (mucho) frío.	I am (very) cold.
Tengo prisa.	I am in a hurry.
Tengo miedo.	I am afraid.
Tiene razón.	He is right.
No tiene razón.	He is wrong.
Tengo sueño.	I am sleepy.

Note also the following idioms:

¿Cuántos años tiene usted?	How old are you?
Tengo veintiocho años.	I am twenty-eight.
Tiene el pelo rubio y los ojos azules.	He has blond hair and blue eyes.
¿Qué tiene usted?	What's the matter with you?
No tengo nada.	Nothing. (*Lit.* I don't have anything.)

Tener que with the infinitive means *to have to, must.*

Usted *tiene que* dejar la propina esta vez.	You *have to* leave the tip this time.
Tenemos que volver temprano.	*We must* return early.

The verb *deber* with the infinitive is very often used to mean *must, should, ought to.*

Usted *debe dejar* dos pesos por lo menos.	You *should leave* at least two pesos.
¿A qué hora *debemos partir?*	At what time *are we supposed to leave?*
Ustedes *deben estudiar* si quieren aprender.	You *ought to study* if you want to learn.

"Acabar de" with the Infinitive

Spanish has a special verb which conveys the idea of the English expression *have just* plus the past participle. This is the present of *acabar de* with the infinitive.

Acabamos de llegar.	We have just arrived.

The Verb "Querer"

The verb *querer* can mean *to want, to wish,* and *to love.*

¿Qué quiere usted?	What do you want?
No quiero buscarlo ahora.	I don't want to look for it now.
Quiero a María y no *quiero* partir sin ella.	I *love* Mary and I don't *want* to leave without her.

A special form of this verb, *quisiera, I should like,* is

more polite than *quiero, I want,* and is often used instead
of it.

Quisiera otra taza de café.	*I should like* another cup of coffee.
Quisiera presentarle a mi tío.	*I'd like* to introduce you to my uncle.

Notice the following idioms:

¿Qué quiere Vd. decir?	What do you mean?
¿Qué quiere decir esta palabra?	What does this word mean?
¿Qué significa esta palabra?	What does this word mean?
Como Vd. quiera.	As you wish.

The Verbs "Saber" and "Conocer"

In English we use the same word, *to know,* for both
knowing facts and knowing people. In Spanish, however, these ideas are separated. *Conocer* means *to know*
in the sense of being acquainted with persons and
places, while *saber* means *to know* facts. *Conocer* may
also mean to meet, to make the acquaintance of. Both
verbs are irregular in the first person singular of the
present. *Saber* has *sé,* and *conocer* has *conozco.*

¿Quién sabe?	Who knows?
Sólo Dios sabe.	Only God knows.
¿Sabe Vd. la fecha?	Do you know the date?
No la conozco, pero quisiera conocerla.	I do not know her, but I'd like to meet her.
Mucho gusto en conocerle.	Pleased to meet you.
Le conocí el año pasado.	I met him last year.

Basic Verbs and Infinitives

In the last few pages dealing with special verbs it has been shown that by combining many verbs with an infinitive we can express a great variety of ideas. Let us mention again some of the most important of these verbs.

ir a	to be going to	
tener que	to have to	
querer	to want to, wish to	and infinitive
poder	to be able to	
deber	to have to, ought to	
acabar de	to have just	and past participle

Here are some more illustrative sentences:

¿Va usted a estudiar?	*Are you going* to study?
Voy a leer el periódico.	*I am going* to read the paper.
Tengo que dejarlo para mañana.	*I have* to leave it for tomorrow.
¿Quiere usted ayudarme?	*Will you* help me?
Quisiera ir al cine.	*I would like* to go to the movies.
No puedo salir hoy.	*I cannot* go out today.
¿Puede usted prestarme cien pesos?	*Can you* lend me a hundred pesos?
Debemos levantarnos temprano.	*We have* to get up early.
Acaban de entrar.	*They have just* come in.

Prepositions and Infinitives

In English we often use the present participle after a preposition (before *leaving*, after *eating*, without *thinking*, etc.) This is never done in Spanish. Only the infinitive form of the verb may follow a preposition.

antes de salir	before leaving
después de llegar	after arriving
para trabajar	in order to work
sin hablar	without speaking
al entrar	on entering

Some Useful Expressions

Here are some useful idiomatic expressions which have not appeared in the main body of this little grammar.

Qué hora es? Son las ocho y media	What time is it? It is 8.30
Echo de menos a mis padres (echar de menos).	I miss my parents. (to miss)
Dar un paseo.	To take a walk. (or a drive)
No importa.	It doesn't matter.
No se preocupe.	Don't trouble yourself. (*or* don't worry)
Lo siento mucho.	I'm very sorry.
Está bien.	O.K., all right.
Es Vd. muy amable.	You're very kind.
Que se divierta.	Have a good time.
¡No me diga!	You don't say!
No sirve.	It's no good.
Buenos días.	Good morning.
Buenas tardes.	Good afternoon.
Buenas noches.	Good evening, good night.
¿Qué tal?	How are you? (to a friend)

Hasta luego.	See you later.
Hasta mañana.	See you tomorrow.
Por la mañana.	In the morning.
Por la tarde.	In the afternoon.
Por la noche.	In the evening.
Pasado mañana.	The day after tomorrow.
Mañana por la mañana.	Tomorrow morning.
A tiempo.	On time.
En seguida.	At once.
Al fin.	At last, finally.
Otra vez.	Again.
En vez de.	Instead of.
Pues.	Well.
Quizás.	Perhaps.
Por eso.	Therefore.
Por lo menos.	At least.
Por supuesto.	Of course.
¡Cómo no!	Of course.
Claro.	Of course.
Todo el mundo.	Everybody.
Con mucho gusto.	With pleasure.
Muchas gracias.	Many thanks.
De nada.	You're welcome.
Con permiso.	Excuse me. (with your permission)
Perdóneme.	Excuse me, pardon me.

Vocabulary Tips

Many words in English and Spanish are exactly the same for both languages. Many others have only minor changes in spelling, and are easily recognized. Study the following vocabulary hints and word lists.

1. Examples of words that are the same in both languages.

color	crisis	drama	error	general
honor	metal	probable	tropical	variable

2. Some words add a final *-e, -a,* or *-o* to the English word.

client*e*	artist*a*	absolut*o*
evident*e*	emblem*a*	contact*o*
ignorant*e*	pianist*a*	defect*o*
important*e*	problem*a*	líquid*o*
part*e*	sistem*a*	pretext*o*

3. The English ending *-ty* is usually the same as the Spanish *-tad* or *-dad.*

ciu*dad*	curiosi*dad*	liber*tad*	socie*dad*

4. English *-y* often corresponds to Spanish *-ía, -ia,* or *-io.*

compañ*ía*	histor*ia*	diccionar*io*
geograf*ía*	farmac*ia*	ordinar*io*

5. English *-tion* equals Spanish *-ción.*

ac*ción*	administra*ción*	fun*ción*

6. English *-ous* is often Spanish *-oso.*

delici*oso*	fam*oso*	gener*oso*	preci*oso*

Vocabulary Building With Cognates

When you study a foreign language, building a vocabulary is often one of the most difficult and laborious tasks. It can mean a great deal of tedious memorization and time-consuming study. Yet an English-speaker is in a fortunate position for learning foreign vocabulary, and his work can be considerably lightened. English is composite in origin, and in its immense word-trove are to be found thousands of forms that are borrowed from other languages. If you have already studied a foreign language, you probably remember the pleasure you felt when you came upon a word that was like its English counterpart; it immediately became easy to remember and use, since it was linked to something familiar, and it probably stayed in your memory longer than other words.

This word list is based upon a useful principle that is not widely used —the seeking out of vocabulary resemblances and making full use of them. It would seem to be obvious that the easiest way to obtain a Spanish vocabulary would be to study words that English shares with Spanish. Yet, surprisingly enough, until this present list, there has been no systematic compilation of the words that form the common ground between English and Spanish.

This list contains more than twenty-four hundred Spanish words, together with an equal number of English words that have the same meaning, and are either identical or very close in spelling to the Spanish. Most of these words are cognates, the Spanish words being derived from Latin, while the comparable English words have come either from literary Latin or indirectly through French or Italian. Some of the words in this list, however, are not cognates, but are simple borrowings. You are probably already familiar with such English borrowings from Spanish in such words as *sombrero*, *fiesta*, and *siesta*. There are probably even more words, like *automóvil*, *eléctrico*, and *tren* (train), which have moved from English into Spanish.

These twenty-four hundred words are the most frequently used words that English and Spanish have in common parallel forms. They are all important words in Spanish, all appearing among the top six thousand words in word-frequency counts. This list has been based upon a study of comparative cognates between English, French, and Spanish, submitted by William E. Johnson, Jr., as a master's thesis to the George Peabody School for Teachers. The editors of Dover Publications have collated it with Helen S. Eaton's *Semantic Frequency List* and have enlarged it accordingly. While this list does not contain all the most common words in Spanish (since there are many Spanish words that do not have parallel English forms), it will give you many of the words that you are likely to need, and will enable you to express your needs in the easiest way.

Do not go beyond the words in this list, however, in assuming that English and Spanish words that look alike have the same meaning. There are many false analogies between the two languages, and it is not always safe to guess at Spanish words because of their appearance. Many words which were once related in the past have since drifted apart in meaning, and in many other words there were simply chance resemblances between English and Spanish. The Spanish word *largo* does not mean large; it means long.

If you concentrate on the twenty-four hundred words of this listing, you will find that you will be able to comprehend a good deal of Spanish, and will be able to express your thoughts with a minimum of memorization. Learn to recast your thoughts in these words when you speak. Instead of thinking (in English) of big and great and large, think of grand, which is close to Spanish *grande*; instead of thinking of minute, think of moment; instead of let, think of permit. Each of these words has its cognate or near equivalent in Spanish, and you will be able to express yourself without ambiguities or misstatements.

Use whatever methods come easiest to you for learning these words. Some language experts advise you simply to read through the list two or three times a day for several weeks, and then to let your mind pick up words unconsciously. The association between English and Spanish in this list is so close, that simply reading and rereading the list will enlarge your vocabulary by hundreds of useful words. Some teachers recommend that you memorize a certain number of words each day, perhaps making sentences with them. There aren't many short cuts to learning and study. This is one of the few of real value. Do not be afraid of making mistakes. You may be unidiomatic at times; you may be grammatically incorrect occasionally; but you will probably be understood.

Table of Common Equivalents

Spanish	English	Examples	
-mente	-ly	absoluta*mente*	absolute*ly*
-dad	-ty	necesi*dad*	necessi*ty*
-ción	-tion	condi*ción*	condi*tion*
-ie- (sometimes)	-e-	mi*e*mbra	m*e*mber
-ue- (sometimes)	-o-	c*ue*rpo	c*o*rpse
v	b	automó*v*il	automo*b*ile
f	ph	*f*rase	*ph*rase

abandon	abandonar	actuate	actuar
abdicate	abdicar	action	acción
abnormal	abnormal	active	activo
abolish	abolir	activity	actividad
abolition	abolición	actor	actor
abominable	abominable	actress	actriz
abound	abundar	actuality	actualidad
abrupt	abrupto	adapt	adaptar
absolute	absoluto	addition	adición
absolutely	absolutamente	adhere	adherir
absorb	absorber	adherent	adherente
abstain	abstener (se)	adjust	ajustar
abstraction	abstracción	administrate	administrar
absurd	absurdo	administration	administración
abundance	abundancia	administrative	administrativo
abundant	abundante	administrator	administrador
abundantly	abundantemente	admirable	admirable
abuse (*n.*)	abuso	admirably	admirablemente
abuse (*v.*)	abusar	admiration	admiración
abyss	abismo	admire	admirar
academy	academia	admit	admitir
accelerate	acelerar	admonish	amonestar
accent	acento	adolescence	adolescencia
accentuate	acentuar	adolescent	adolescente
acceptance	aceptación	adopt	adoptar
access	acceso	adoption	adopción
accessory	accesorio	adoration	adoración
accident	accidente	adore	adorar
acclaim (*v.*)	aclamar	adulation	adulación
accompany	acompañar	adult (*adj.*) (*n.*)	adulto
accord (*n.*)	acuerdo	advance (*n.*)	avance
accumulate	acumular	advance (*v.*)	avanzar
accusation	acusación	adventure	aventura
accuse	acusar	adventurer	aventurero
accustom	acostumbrar	adverb	adverbio
acid	ácido	adversary	adversario
acquire	adquirir	adverse	adverso
acquisition	adquisición	adversity	adversidad
act (*n.*)	acto	aesthetic	estético
act (*v.*)	actuar	affable	afable

affect (v.)	afectar	amber	ámbar
affection	afección	ambition	ambición
affirm	afirmar	ambitious	ambicioso
affirmation	afirmación	ameliorate	ameliorar
affirmative	afirmativo	American	americano
affliction	aflicción	amiability	amabilidad
agency	agencia	amicable	amigable
agent	agente	amplify	amplificar
aggravate	agravar	analogous	análogo
aggregate (v.)	agregar	analogy	analogía
aggression	agresión	analysis	análisis
aggressive	agresivo	analyze	analizar
aggressor	agresor	anarchy	anarquía
agile	ágil	anecdote	anécdota
agitate	agitar	angel	ángel
agitation	agitación	angle	ángulo
agony	agonía	anguish	angustia
agreeable	agradable	animal	animal
agricultural	agrícola	animate	animar
agriculture	agricultura	animation	animación
ah!	¡ah!	annex (n.)	anexo
air (n.)	aire	anniversary	aniversario
alarm (v.)	alarmar	announce	anunciar
album	álbum	annual	anual
alcohol	alcohol	annul	anular
alcoholic	alcohólico	anonymous	anónimo
alert	alerta	antecedent	antecedente
align	alinear	anterior	anterior
aliment	alimento	anticipate	anticipar
alimentation	alimentación	antique	antiquo
allege	alegar	antiquity	antigüedad
alleviate	aliviar	aplomb	aplomo
alliance	alianza	apostle	apóstol
allusion	alusión	apostolic	apostólico
altar	altar	apparatus	aparato
alter	alterar	apparent	aparente
alteration	alteración	apparition	aparición
alternate (v.)	alternar	appeal (v.)	apelar
alternately	alternativamente	appear	aparecer
amass	amasar	appendix	apéndice

appetite	apetito	aspect	aspecto
applaud	aplaudir	aspiration	aspiración
applause	aplauso	aspire	aspirar
applicable	aplicable	assassin	asesino
application	aplicación	assassinate	asesinar
apply	aplicar	assembly	asamblea
apprehension	aprehensión	assimilate	asimilar
apprentice	aprendiz	assistance	asistencia
approbation	aprobación	associate (v.)	asociar
appropriate (v.)	apropiar	association	asociación
approve	aprobar	assume	asumir
approximate	aproximar	astronomer	astrónomo
aptitude	aptitud	athlete	atleta
arbitrariness	arbitrariedad	athletic	atlético
arbitrary	arbitrario	atmosphere	atmósfera
arbitrator	arbitrador	atom	átomo
arcade	arcada	atrocity	atrocidad
arch	arco	attack (n.)	ataque
archipelago	archipiélago	attack (v.)	atacar
architect	arquitecto	attention	atención
architecture	arquitectura	attentive	atento
ardor	ardor	attentively	atentivamente
ardorous	ardoroso	attenuate	atenuar
argument	argumento	attic	ático
arid	árido	attitude	actitud
aristocracy	aristocracia	attraction	atracción
aristocratic	aristocrático	attractive	atractivo
arm (v.)	armar	attribute (n.)	atributo
aroma	aroma	attribute (v.)	atribuir
arrogance	arrogancia	audacious	audaz
arrogant	arrogante	audacity	audacia
art	arte	audience	audiencia
article	artículo	augment	aumentar
articulate	articular	augmentation	aumentación
articulation	articulación	august	augusto
artificial	artificial	aurora	aurora
artillery	artillería	austere	austero
artist	artista	austerity	austeridad
artistic	artístico	authentic	auténtico
ascend	ascender	author	autor
ascension	ascensión	authority	autoridad

authorization	autorización
authorize	autorizar
automatic	automático
automaton	autómata
automobile	automóvil
autonomy	autonomía
auxiliary	auxiliar
avarice	avaricia
avenue	avenida
aversion	aversión
avid	ávido
azure	azur
bah!	¡bah!
balance (n.)	balanza
balance (v.)	balancear
balcony	balcón
balloon	balón
band	banda
bandit	bandido
bank	banco
banker	banquero
banquet	banquete
bar	barra
barbarian	bárbaro
barbarity	barbaridad
barber	barbero
bark	barca
baron	barón
barrel	barril
base	base
bastard	bastardo
battalion	batallón
battery	batería
battle	batalla
bayonet	bayoneta
benediction	bendición
benefice	beneficio
beneficent	benéfico
benefit (n.)	beneficio

benefit (v.)	beneficiar
benevolence	benevolencia
benevolent	benévolo
benign	benigno
biblical	bíblico
bicycle	bicicleta
biography	biografía
bland	blando
blasphemy	blasfemia
blouse	blusa
boat	bote
bomb	bomba
border	borde
boulevard	bulevar
bourgeois	burgués
boxer	boxeador
brave	bravo
bravely	bravamente
bravery	bravura
bravo	bravo
brigade	brigada
brilliant	brillante
britannic	británico
bronze	bronce
brutal	brutal
brutality	brutalidad
brutally	brutalmente
brute	bruto
burlesque	burlesco
bust	busto
cable	cable
cabriolet	cabriolé
cadaver	cadáver
cafe	café
calculate	calcular
calculation	cálculo
calendar	calendario
calm (v.)	calmar
calumny	calumnia
calvary	calvario

camel	camello	central	central
canal	canal	ceremony	ceremonia
canape	canapé	certificate	certificado
canary	canario	champagne	champaña
candid	cándido	champion	campeón
candidacy	candidatura	chaos	caos
candidate	candidato	character	carácter
candor	candor	characteristic	característico
canon	canón	characterize	caracterizar
canton	cantón	charity	caridad
capacity	capacidad	chastity	castidad
cape	capa	chauffeur	chauffeur
capital	capital	check (n.)	cheque
caprice	capricho	chic	chic
capricious	caprichoso	chimney	chimenea
captain	capitán	chocolate	chocolate
capture	capturar	christian	cristiano
caravan	caravana	chronicle	crónica
cardinal	cardinal	cigar	cigarro
career	carrera	cigarette	cigarillo
carpenter	carpintero	circle	círculo
carton	cartón	circuit	circuito
cascade	cascada	circular (adj.)	circular
case	caso	circulate	circular
caste	casta	circulation	circulación
castigate	castigar	circumstance	circunstancia
casual	casual	circus	circo
catalogue	catálogo	citation	citación
catastrophe	catástrofe	cite	citar
category	categoría	civilization	civilización
cathedral	catedral	civilize	civilizar
catholic	católico	class	clase
catholicism	catolicismo	classic	clásico
cause (n.)	causa	classify	clasificar
cause (v.)	causar	clemence	clemencia
cease	cesar	clement	clemente
cede	ceder	client	cliente
celebrate	celebrar	clientele	clientela
celestial	celeste	climate	clima
cement	cemento	club	club
center	centro	code	código

cohesion	cohesión	comparison	comparación
coincide	coincidir	compassion	compasión
coincidence	coincidencia	compatriot	compatriota
collaborate	colaborar	compensation	compensación
collaboration	colaboración	complement	complemento
collaborator	colaborador	complete (*adj.*)	completo
colleague	colega	complete (*v.*)	completar
collection	colección	completely	completamente
collectivity	colectividad	complex	complejo
colonial	colonial	complicate	complicar
colony	colonia	complicated	complicado
color (*n.*)	color	complication	complicación
color (*v.*)	colorar	complicity	complicidad
colored	colorado	compliment	complimento
colossal	colosal	comport (*v.*)	comportar
colossus	coloso	composition	composición
column	columna	comprehend	comprender
combat (*n.*)	combate	compromise (*n.*)	compromiso
combat (*v.*)	combatir	comrade	camarada
combination	combinación	concede	conceder
combine	combinar	conceive	concebir
combustion	combustión	concentrate	concentrar
comedian	comediante	concentration	concentración
comedy	comedia	concept	concepto
comical	cómico	conception	concepción
commandant	comandante	concert	concierto
commence	comenzar	concession	concesión
commentary	comentario	conciliate	conciliar
commerce	comercio	conciliation	conciliación
commercial	comercial	conclude	concluir
commissary	comisario	conclusion	conclusión
commission	comisión	concourse	concurso
commit	cometer	concrete	concreto
common	común	concurrence	concurrencia
communicate	comunicar	condemnation	condenación
communication	comunicación	condense	condensar
communion	comunión	condition	condición
community	comunidad	conduct (*n.*)	conducta
company	compañía	conductor	conductor
comparable	comparable	confederation	confederación
compare	comparar	confer	conferir

conference	conferencia	consul (*n.*)	cónsul
confess	confesar	consult	consultar
confession	confesión	consume	consumir
confessor	confesor	consummation	consumación
confidence	confianza	contact	contacto
confident (*n.*)	confidente	contagious	contagioso
confidential	confidencial	contain	contener
confine (*v.*)	confinar	contaminate	contaminar
confirm	confirmar	contemplate	contemplar
confirmation	confirmación	contemplation	contemplación
conflict	conflicto	contemporary	contemporáneo
conform	conforme	contend	contender
confusion	confusión	content	contento
congress	congreso	continent	continente
conjure	conjurar	continual	continuo
conquer	conquistar	continually	continuamente
conquest	conquista	continuation	continuación
conscience	conciencia	continue	continuar
consecration	consagración	contract	contrato
consent (*n.*)	consentimiento	contraction	contracción
consent (*v.*)	consentir	contradict	contradecir
consequence	consecuencia	contradiction	contradicción
conservation	conservación	contrarily	contrariamente
conserve	conservar	contrary	contrario
consider	considerar	contrast (*n.*)	contraste
considerable	considerable	contrast (*v.*)	contrastar
consideration	consideración	contribute	contribuir
consign	consignar	contribution	contribución
consist	consistir	control (*n.*)	control
consolation	consolación	convention	convención
console	consolar	conversation	conversación
consolidate	consolidar	converse (*v.*)	conversar
consonant	consonante	conversion	conversión
conspirator	conspirador	convert (*n.*)	converto
conspire	conspirar	convert (*v.*)	convertir
constant	constante	conviction	eonvicción
constitute	constituir	convince	convencer
constitution	constitución	convoke	convocar
constitutional	constitucional	cooperative	cooperativa
construct	construir	copious	copioso
construction	construción	copy (*n.*)	copia

copy (v.)	copiar	curious	curioso
coral	coral	curve	curva
cordial	cordial	cylinder	cilindro
corporation	corporación	cypress	ciprés
correct (adj.)	correcto		
correction	corrección		
correctly	correctamente	dame	dama
correspond	corresponder	dance (n.)	danza
correspondence	correspondencia	dance (v.)	danzar
correspondent	correspondiente	date (v.)	datar
corridor	corredor	debate	debate
corruption	corrupción	debilitate	debilitar
cost (v.)	costar	debut	debut
count (v.)	contar	decade	década
course	curso	decadence	decadencia
courtesy	cortesía	decent	decente
cranium	cráneo	deception	decepción
cream	crema	decide	decidir
create	crear	decidedly	decididamente
creation	creación	decision	decisión
creator	creador	decisive	decisivo
creature	criatura	declaration	declaración
credit	crédito	declare	declarar
crepuscule	crepúsculo	decline	declinar
crest	cresta	decorate	decorar
crime	crimen	decoration	decoración
criminal	criminal	decree	decreto
crisis	crisis	dedicate	dedicar
critic	crítico	deduction	deducción
criticism	crítica	defect	defecto
crude	crudo	defective	defectuoso
cruel	cruel	defend	defender
cruelly	cruelmente	defense	defensa
crystal	cristal	define	definir
Cuban	cubano	definite	definitivo
cube	cubo	definition	definición
cultivate	cultivar	degenerate	degenerar
cultivator	cultivador	delegation	delegación
culture	cultura	deliberate	deliberar
cupola	cúpula	delicacy	delicadeza
curiosity	curiosidad	delicate	delicado

delicious	delicioso	devastate	devastar
delinquent	delincuente	devotion	devoción
delirium	delirio	devour	devorar
democracy	democracia	devout	devoto
democratic	democrático	dialogue	diálogo
demolish	demoler	diameter	diámetro
demon	demonio	diamond	diamante
demonstrate	demonstrar	dictate	dictar
demonstration	demonstración	dictionary	diccionario
denote	denotar	difference	diferencia
denounce	denunciar	different	diferente
dense	denso	difficult	difícil
density	densidad	difficultly	difícilmente
denude	desnudar	difficulty (*n.*)	dificultad
department	departamento	diffusion	difusión
dependence	dependencia	digestion	digestión
deplorable	deplorable	dignity	dignidad
deplore	deplorar	diligence	diligencia
deposit	depositar	dimension	dimensión
despotism	despotismo	diocese	diócesis
derive	derivar	diplomatic	diplomático
descend	descender	direct	directo
describe	describir	direction	dirección
description	descripción	directly	directamente
desert (*n.*)	desierto	director	director
desert (*v.*)	desertar	disagreeable	desagradable
designate	designar	disarm	desarmar
desire (*v.*)	desear	disaster	desastre
desist	desistir	disc	disco
despair	desesperar	discern	discernir
desperation	desesperación	disciple	discípulo
despot	déspota	discipline	disciplina
destination	destinación	disconcert	desconcertar
destine	destinar	disconsolate	desconsolado
destiny	destino	discontent	descontento
destroy	destrozar	discord	discordia
destruction	destrucción	discourse	discurso
detail	detalle	discreet	discreto
determine	determinar	discreetly	discretamente
detestable	detestable	discretion	discreción
detriment	detrimento	discuss	discutir

discussion	discusión	domination	dominación
disembark	desembarcar	dormitory	dormitorio
disfavorable	desfavorable	double (adj.)	doble
disgrace	desgracia	double (v.)	doblar
disgust (v.)	disgustar	dragon	dragón
dishonor (n.)	deshonor	drama	drama
disorder (n.)	desorden	dramatic	dramático
dispatch	despacho	duel	duelo
dispense	dispensar	duke	duque
disperse	dispersar	durable	durable
disposition	disposición	duration	duración
dispute (n.)	disputa	dynasty	dinastía
dispute (v.)	disputar		
dissolution	disolución	ebullition	ebulición
dissolve	disolver	eccentric	excéntrico
distance	distancia	eccentricity	excentricidad
distant	distante	ecclesiastical	eclesiástico
distillation	destilación	echo	eco
distillery	destilería	economic	económico
distinct	distinto	economy	economía
distinction	distinción	edict	edicto
distinguish	distinguir	edifice	edificio
distraction	distracción	edify	edificar
distribute	distribuir	edition	edición
distribution	distribución	education	educación
divan	diván	effect	efecto
divergence	divergencia	effective	efectivo
diversion	diversión	efficacy	eficacia
divert	divertir	effusion	efusión
divine (n.)	divino	egoism	egoísmo
divine (v.)	adivinar	egoist	egoísta
division	división	elaboration	elaboración
divorce (v.)	divorciar	elastic	elástico
divulge	divulgar	election	elección
docile	dócil	elector	elector
doctor	doctor	electoral	electoral
doctrine	doctrina	electric	eléctrico
document	documento	electricity	electricidad
dogma	dogma	elegance	elegancia
domicile	domicilio	elegant	elegante
dominate	dominar	element	elemento

elevate	elevar	errant	errante
elevation	elevación	error	error
eliminate	eliminar	erudition	erudición
eloquence	elocuencia	essence	esencia
eloquent	elocuente	essential	esencial
emanate	emanar	essentially	esencialmente
emancipate	emancipar	establish	establecer
embalm	embalsamar	establishment	establecimiento
embark	embarcar	estimable	estimable
emblem	emblema	eternal	eterno
emigrant	emigrante	eternally	eternamente
emigration	emigración	eternity	eternidad
eminent	eminente	eternize	eternizar
emotion	emoción	evacuate	evacuar
emperor	emperador	evade	evadir
emphasis	énfasis	evaluate	evaluar
empire	imperio	eventual	eventual
enemy	enemigo	evidence	evidencia
energetic	enérgico	evident	evidente
energetically	enérgicamente	evidently	evidentemente
energy	energía	evoke	evocar
enervate	enervar	evolution	evolución
engender	engendrar	exact	exacto
enigma	enigma	exactitude	exactitud
enormous	enorme	exactly	exactamente
enter	entrar	exaggerate	exagerar
enthusiasm	entusiasmo	exaggeration	exageración
enthusiast	entusiasta	exalt	exaltar
entitle	intitular	exaltation	exaltación
enumerate	enumerar	examination	examen
envy	envidia	examine	examinar
epicure	epicúreo	excellence	excelencia
episode	episodio	excellent	excelente
epoch	época	except	excepto
equality	igualdad	exception	excepción
equilibrate	equilibrar	exceptional	excepcional
equilibrium	equilibrio	exceptionally	excepcionalmente
equity	equidad	excess	exceso
equivalent	equivalente	excessive	excesivo
era	era	excessively	excesivamente
err	errar	excitation	excitación

excite	excitar	exterior	exterior
exclamation	exclamación	extinguish	extinguir
exclude	excluir	extra	extra
exclusive	exclusivo	extract	extracto
exclusively	exclusivamente	extraction	extracción
excursion	excursión	extraordinary	extraordinario
excuse (n.)	excusa	extreme	extremo
excuse (v.)	excusar	extremity	extremidad
executor	ejecutor		
exemption	exempción	fable	fábula
exhibit (v.)	exhibir	fabricate	fabricar
exhibition	exhibición	fabrication	fabricación
exigency	exigencia	fabulous	fabuloso
exist (v.)	existir	facilitate	facilitar
existence	existencia	facility	facilidad
exotic	exótico	faction	facción
expansion	expansión	factor	factor
expansive	expansivo	faculty	facultad
expedition	expedición	false	falso
expel	expulsar	falsify	falsear
experience	experiencia	falsity	falsedad
experiment (v.)	experimentar	fame	fama
experimental	experimental	familiarity	familiaridad
expert	experto	family	familia
expiation	expiación	famous	famoso
expire	expirar	fanaticism	fanatismo
explication	explicación	fantastic	fantástico
exploit (v.)	explotar	fantasy	fantasía
exploitation	explotación	fascinate	fascinar
exploration	exploración	fatality	fatalidad
explore	explorar	fatigue	fatiga
explosion	explosión	fatuous	fatuo
exportation	exportación	favor (n.)	favor
exposition	exposición	favor (v.)	favorecer
express (n.)	expreso	favorable	favorable
express (v.)	expresar	favorite (n., adj.)	favorito
expression	expresión	fecund	fecundo
expressive	expresivo	federation	federación
expulsion	expulsión	felicitate	felicitar
exquisite	exquisito	felicitation	felicitación
extension	extensión	felicity	felicidad

LIST OF COGNATES

feminine	femenino	fragment	fragmento
ferment (v.)	fermentar	fragrance	fragancia
ferocious	feroz	frank	franco
ferocity	ferocidad	frankly	francamente
fertile	fértil	frenetic	frenético
fervent	ferviente	frequent (adj.)	frecuente
fervor	fervor	frequent (v.)	frecuentar
festive	festivo	frequently	frecuentemente
fiber	fibra	fresh	fresco
fiction	ficción	frivolity	frivolidad
fidelity	fidelidad	frivolous	frívolo
figure (n.)	figura	frontier	frontera
filial	filial	fruit	fruta
final	final	fruiterer	frutero
finally	finalmente	frustrate	frustrar
finance	finanza	fugitive	fugitivo
financial	financiero	function (n.)	función
fine	fino	function (v.)	funcionar
finis	fin	functionary	funcionario
firm (adj.)	firme	fundament	fundamento
firmament	firmamento	fundamental	fundamental
flagrant	flagrante	funeral	funeral
flexibility	flexibilidad	furious	furioso
float	flotar	furtive	furtivo
fluid	flúido		
foment	fomentar	fury	{furia / furor}
force (v.)	forzar		
forced	forzado		
form (n.)	forma	gallant	galante
form (v.)	formar	gallery	galería
formality	formalidad	gallop	galope
formation	formación	gardener	jardinero
formidable	formidable	gas	gas
formula	formula	gasoline	gasolina
formulate	formular	gendarme	gendarme
fortify	fortificar	general (n.)	general
fortunate	afortunado	general (adj.)	general
fortune	fortuna	generality	generalidad
foundation	fundación	generalize	generalizar
fraction	fracción	generally	generalmente
fragile	frágil	generation	generación

generosity	generosidad	guillotine	guillotina
generous	generoso	guitar	guitarra
genius	génio	gusto	gusto
genteel	gentil	gymnasium	gimnasio
gentility	gentileza	gyrate	girar
genuine	genuino		
geography	geografía	habit	hábito
geometrical	geométrico	habitation	habitación
geranium	geranio	habitual	habitual,
germ	germen	habitually	habitualmente
germinate	germinar	hatchet	hacha
gesticulate	gesticular	harmonious	armonioso
gesture	gesto	harmony	armonía
giant	gigante	heir	heredero
gigantic	gigantesco	hemisphere	hemisferio
glacial	glacial	herb	hierba
globe	globo	heresy	herejía
glorious	glorioso	heretic	herético
glory	gloria	hereditary	hereditario
golf	golf	hero	héroe
gothic	gótico	heroic	heróico
gourmet	gourmet	heroism	heroísmo
gracious	gracioso	historian	historiador
gradual	gradual	historic	histórico
graduate (v.)	graduar	history	historia
grain	grano	homicide	homicidio
grammar	gramática	homogeneous	homogéneo
grandeur	grandeza	honest	honesto
granite	granito	honesty	honestidad
graphic	gráfico	honor	honor
gratify	gratificar	honorable	honorable
gratis	gratis	horizon	horizonte
gratitude	gratitud	horizontal	horizontal
grave (adj.)	grave	horrendous	horrendo
gravely	gravemente	horrible	horrible
grotesque	grotesco	horribly	horriblemente
group (n.)	grupo	horror	horror
group (v.)	agrupar	hospital	hospital
guarantee (n.)	garantía	hospitality	hospitalidad
guarantee (v.)	garantizar	hostile	hostil
guard (n.)	guardia		

hostility	hostilidad	imminent	inminente
hotel	hotel	immobility	inmovilidad
human	humano	immolate	inmolar
humanity	humanidad	immortal	inmortal
humid	húmedo	impartial	imparcial
humiliate	humillar	impassible	impasible
humiliation	humillación	impatience	impaciencia
humility	humildad	imperative	imperativo
humor	humor	imperceptible	imperceptible
hurricane	huracán	imperfect	imperfecto
hydrogen	hidrógeno	imperial	imperial
hygiene	higiene	impertinence	impertinencia
hypocrisy	hipocresía	impetuous	impetuoso
hypocrite	hipócrita	implacable	implacable
hysterical	histérico	implicate	implicar
		implore	implorar
idea	idea	import (*v.*)	importar
ideal	ideal	importance	importancia
identical	idéntico	important	importante
identity	identidad	importation	importación
idiot	idiota	importunate	importuno
ignoble	innoble	imposition	imposición
ignorance	ignorancia	impossibility	imposibilidad
ignorant	ignorante	impossible	imposible
illuminate	iluminar	impotence	impotencia
illusion	ilusión	impotent	impotente
illustrate	ilustrar	impregnate	impregnar
illustration	ilustración	impression	impresión
illustrous	ilustre	improvise	improvisar
image	imagen	imprudence	imprudencia
imaginary	imaginario	imprudent	imprudente
imagination	imaginación	impudent	impudente
imaginative	imaginativo	impulsion	impulsión
imagine	imaginar	impure	impuro
imbecile	imbécil	inaugurate	inaugurar
imitate	imitar	incapacity	incapacidad
imitation	imitación	incessant	incesante
immediate	inmediato	incident	incidente
immediately	inmediatamente	inclination	inclinación
immense	inmenso	incline (*v.*)	inclinar (se)
immensity	inmensidad	incomparable	incomparable

incompatible	incompatible	infantile	infantil
incomplete	incompleto	infantry	infantería
incomprehensible	incomprensible	inferior	inferior
incontestable	incontestable	infernal	infernal
inconvenient	inconveniente	inferno	infierno
incorporate	incorporar	infinitely	infinitamente
incredible	increíble	infinity	infinidad
incurable	incurable	influence (n.)	influencia
indecision	indecisión	influence (v.)	influir
indefatigable	infatigable	influential	influente
indefinite	indefinido	inform (v.)	informar
independence	independencia	information	información
independent	independiente	ingenious	ingenioso
Indian	indiano	ingratitude	ingratitud
indicate	indicar	inhuman	inhumano
indication	indicación	initial	inicial
indicative	indicativo	initative	iniciativo
indifference	indiferencia	injury	injuria
indifferent	indiferente	injustice	injusticia
indigenous	indígena	innocence	inocencia
indignation	indignación	innocent	inocente
indirect	indirecto	inoffensive	inofensivo
indiscreet	indiscreto	insane	insano
indiscretion	indiscreción	inscription	inscripción
indispensable	indispensable	insect	insecto
individual (n.)	individuo	insensible	insensible
individual (adj.)	individual	inseparable	inseparable
indolence	indolencia	insert	insertar
indulgence	indulgencia	insignificant	insignificante
indulgent	indulgente	insinuate	insinuar
industrial	industrial	insist	insistir
industry	industria	insistence	insistencia
inert	inerte	insolence	insolencia
inestimable	inestimable	insolent	insolente
inevitable	inevitable	inspection	inspección
inexplicable	inexplicable	inspector	inspector
inextricable	inextricable	inspiration	inspiración
infallible	infalible	inspire	inspirar
infamous	infame	install	instalar
infamy	infamia	installation	instalación
infancy	infancia	instance	instancia

instantaneously	instantáneamente	intervention	intervención
instinct	instinto	interview	interviú
instinctive	instintivo	intimacy	intimidad
instinctively	instintivamente	intimate	íntimo
institute (n.)	instituto	intimidate	intimidar
institute (v.)	instituir	intolerable	intolerable
institution	institución	intonation	intonación
instruction	instrucción	intrepid	intrépido
instrument	instrumento	intrigue	intriga
insufficiency	insuficiencia	introduce	introducir
insufficient	insuficiente	introduction	introducción
insular	insular	intuition	intuición
insult (n.)	insulto	inundate	inundar
insult (v.)	insultar	invade	invadir
insuperable	insuperable	invariable	invariable
insupportable	insoportable	invasion	invasión
insurgent	insurgente	invent	inventar
intact	intacto	invention	invención
integral	integral	inverse	inverso
integrity	integridad	investigate	investigar
intellectual	intelectual	investigation	investigación
intelligence	inteligencia	invisible	invisible
intelligent	inteligente	invitation	invitación
intense	intenso	invite	invitar
intensity	intensidad	invoke	invocar
intent	intento	involuntary	involuntario
intention	intención	iris	iris
interest (n.)	interés	ironical	irónico
interest (v.)	interesar (se)	irony	ironía
interior	interior	irregular	irregular
interminable	interminable	irreparable	irreparable
international	internacional	irresistible	irresistible
interpellation	interpelación	irresolute	irresoluto
interpret	interpretar	irritate	irritar
interpretation	interpretación	irritation	irritación
interpreter	intérprete	irruption	irrupción
interrogate	interrogar	isle	isla
interrupt	interrumpir		
interruption	interrupción		
interval	intervalo	jar	jarra
intervene	intervenir	jargon	jerga

jubilance	júbilo	limit	limitar
judicial	judicial	limitation	limitación
judiciary	judiciario	limpid	límpido
jurisdiction	jurisdicción	line	línea
jurisprudence	jurisprudencia	liquid	líquida
just	justo	liquidate	liquidar
justice	justicia	liquor	licor
justify	justificar	list	lista
juvenile (*adj.*)	juvenil	literary	literario
		literature	literatura
		livid	lívido
kilogram	kilogramo	locality	localidad
kilometer	kilómetro	locomotive	locomotora
		logical	lógico
labor (*n.*)	labor	longitude	longitud
labor (*v.*)	laborar	lucid	lúcido
laboratory	laboratorio	lugubrious	lúgubre
laborious	laborioso	luminous	luminoso
labyrinth	laberinto	lyric	lírico
laic	laico		
lament	lamentar		
lamentable	lamentable	magic	mágico
lamp	lámpara	magistrate	magistrado
lance	lanza	magnetic	magnético
language	{ lengua / lenguaje	magnificent	magnífico
		magnitude	magnitud
languid	lánguido	majestic	majestuoso
lassitude	lasitud	majesty	majestad
latitude	latitud	malediction	maldición
laudable	laudable	malice	malicia
laurel	laurel	malignant	maligno
legal	legal	mamma	mamá
legion	legión	mandamus	mandamiento
legislation	legislación	mandate	mandato
legislator	legislador	mania	manía
legitimate	legítimo	manifest (*n.*)	manifiesto
legume	legumbre	manifest (*v.*)	manifestar
liberal	liberal	manifestation	manifestación
liberate	liberar	manner	manera
liberation	liberación	mansion	mansión
liberty	libertad	manual	manual

manuscript	manuscrito	merit	mérito
map	mapa	metal	metal
march (v.)	marchar	metallic	metálico
margin	margen	meteor	meteoro
marine	marino	meter	metro
maritime	marítimo	methodic	metódico
mark (n.)	marca	meticulous	meticuloso
mark (v.)	marcar	metropolis	metrópoli
martyr (n.)	mártir	militarily	militarmente
marvel	maravilla	military	militar
marvelous	maravilloso	militia	milicia
mask	máscara	million	millón
mass	masa	mine (n.)	mina
match (sports)	match	miner	minero
material (adj.)	material	mineral	mineral
maternal	materno	miniature	miniatura
mathematical	matemático	minimum	mínimo
matrimony	matrimonio	ministry	ministro
matron	matrona	minority	minoría
maximum	máximo	minute	minuto
mechanical	mecánico	miserable	miserable
mechanism	mecanismo	misery	miseria
medal	medalla	mission	misión
median	media	mix	mixto
mediate	mediar	mobile	móvil
medicine	medicina	mobilize	movilizar
mediocrity	mediocridad	mode	moda
meditate	meditar	model	modelo
mediation	meditación	moderate (v.)	moderar
melancholic	melancólico	moderation	moderación
melancholy	melancolía	modern	moderno
melody	melodía	modest	modesto
melon	melón	modesty	modestia
member	miembro	modification	modificación
memorable	memorable	modify	modificar
memory	memoria	mold	molde
mental	mental	moment	momento
mentally	mentalmente	momentarily	momentáneamente
mention (v.)	mencionar	momentary	momentáneo
menu	menú	monarch	monarca
mercantile	mercantil	monastery	monasterio

money	moneda	mystic	místico
monologue	monólogo	mystification	mistificación
monopoly	monopolio		
monosyllable	monosílabo	narrate	narrar
monotonous	monótono	narration	narración
monotony	monotonía	nascent	naciente
monster	monstruo	natal	natal
monstrous	monstruoso	nation	nación
monument	monumento	national	nacional
monumental	monumental	nationality	nacionalidad
moral	moral	native	nativo
moralist	moralista	natural	natural
morality	moralidad	naturally	naturalmente
morbid	morboso	naval	naval
moribund	moribundo	navigable	navegable
mortal	mortal	navigation	navegación
mortify	mortificar	necessarily	necesariamente
motivate	motivar	necessary	necesario
motive	motivo	necessitate	necesitar
motor	motor	necessity	necesidad
mount (n.)	monte	negative	negativo
mountain	montaña	negligence	negligencia
movable	movible	negligent	negligente
move (n.)	mover	negotiation	negociación
movement	movimiento	Negro	negro
multiple	múltiple	nerve	nervio
multiply	multiplicar	nervous	nervioso
multitude	multitud	neutral	neutro
mundane	mundano	no	no
municipal	municipal	noble (adj.)	noble
municipality	municipalidad	nocturnal	nocturno
murmur (n.)	murmurio	nomination	nominación
murmur (v.)	murmurar	normal	normal
muscle	músculo	north	norte
museum	museo	notable	notable
music	música	notary	notario
muslin	muselina	note (n.)	nota
mutilate	mutilar	note (v.)	notar
mutual	mutuo	notice (n.)	noticia
mysterious	misterioso	notify	notificar
mystery	mistério	notion	noción

notorious	notorio	omit	omitir
novel (*n.*)	novela	omnibus	ómnibus
novelist	novelista	omnipotent	omnipotente
nucleus	núcleo	opera	ópera
number	número	operate	operar
nutrition	nutrición	operation	operación
		opinion	opinión
oasis	oasis	opportunity	oportunidad
obedience	obediencia	opposition	oposición
obedient	obediente	oppression	opresión
obelisk	obelisco	optic	óptico
object	objeto	optimism	optimismo
objection	objeción	optimist	optimista
objective	objetivo	opulence	opulencia
obligation	obligación	oracle	oráculo
obligatory	obligatorio	oration	oración
oblige	obligar	orator	orador
oblique	oblicuo	orchestra	orquesta
obscure	obscuro	ordinary	ordinario
obscurity	obscuridad	organic	orgánico
observe	observar	organism	organismo
observer	observador	organization	organización
obstacle	obstáculo	organize	organizar
obstinacy	obstinación	orgy	orgía
obstruct	obstruir	orifice	orificio
obtain	obtener	origin	origen
occasion	ocasión	original	original
occupation	ocupación	originality	originalidad
occupy	ocupar (se)	ornament	ornamento
occur	ocurrir	orthography	ortografía
occurrence	ocurrencia	oscillate	oscilar
ocean	océano	ostentation	ostentación
odious	odioso	overture	obertura
offend	ofender	oxygen	oxígeno
offense	ofensa		
offensive	ofensiva	pacific	pacífico
offer	oferta	pact	pacto
office	oficio	pagan	pagano
officially	oficialmente	page	página
olive	oliva	palace	palacio
omission	omisión	pallid	pálido

palm	palma	pensive	pensativo
palpitate	palpitar	penumbra	penumbra
panic	pánico	perceptible	perceptible
panorama	panorama	perfect (v.)	perfeccionar
papa	papá	perfection	perfección
paradise	paraíso	perfectly	perfectamente
parallel	paralelo	perfidious	pérfido
paralyze	paralizar	perfume (v.)	perfumar
pardon (n.)	perdón	period	período
pardon (v.)	perdonar	periodic	periódico
parliamentary	parlamentario	permanent	permanente
part	parte	permission	permiso
partial	parcial	permit (n.)	permiso
participate	participar	permit (v.)	permitir
participation	participación	perpetual	perpetuo
particular (adj.)	particular	persecution	persecución
particularly	particularmente	persevere	perseverar
pass (v.)	pasar	persist	persistir
passion	pasión	person	persona
passive	pasivo	personal	personal
past	pasado	personality	personalidad
paste	pasta	personally	personalmente
pastor	pastor	perspective	perspectiva
paternal	paterno	perspicacious	perspicaz
pathetic	patético	persuade	persuadir
patience	paciencia	perturb	perturbar
patio	patio	perverse	perverso
patriarch	patriarca	perversity	perversidad
patriot	patriota	pest	peste
patriotism	patriotismo	petal	pétalo
patron	patrón	petition	petición
pause	pausa	petroleum	petróleo
pavement	pavimento	pharmacy	farmacia
pearl	perla	phenomena	fenómeno
pedagogue	pedagogo	philosopher	filósofo
pedant	pedante	philosophical	filosófico
pedestal	pedestal	philosophy	filosofía
pendulum	péndulo	phosphorus	fósforo
penetrate	penetrar	photograph	fotografía
peninsula	península	photograph (v.)	fotografiar
pension	pensión	phrase	frase

physical	físico	possibility	posibilidad
piano	piano	possible	posible
piety	piedad	postal	postal
pilot	piloto	posterity	posteridad
pine	pino	potency	potencia
pipe	pipa	practical	práctico
pirate	pirata	practically	prácticamente
pistol	pistola	practice (n.)	práctica
placid	plácido	practice (v.)	practicar
plague	plaga	preamble	preámbulo
plan	plan	precaution	precaución
plane	plano	precede	preceder
planet	planeta	precedent	precedente
plant (n.)	planta	precept	precepto
plant (v.)	plantar	precious	precioso
plastic	plástico	precipice	precipicio
plate (n.)	plato	precipitate	precipitar
plate (v.)	platear	precipitation	precipitación
plenitude	plenitud	precisely	precisamente
poem	poema	precision	precisión
poet	poeta	precursor	precursor
poetical	poético	predecessor	predecesor
poetry	poesía	predominance	predominancia
polar	polar	prefect	prefecto
pole	polo	prefecture	prefectura
polemic	polémica	prefer	preferir
police	policía	preferable	preferible
political	político	preference	preferencia
pomp	pompa	prejudiced	prejuicio
pompous	pomposo	prelate	prelado
ponder	ponderar	preliminary	preliminar
popular	popular	premature	prematuro
popularity	popularidad	preoccupation	preocupación
populous	populoso	preoccupied	preocupado
porcelain	porcelana	preparation	preparación
port	puerto	preposition	preposición
portal	portal	prerogative	prerrogativa
portion	porción	prescribe	prescribir
position	posición	presence	presencia
positive	positivo	present (v.)	presentar
possession	posesión	presentation	presentación

presentiment	presentimiento	progress	progreso
preserve	preservar	progressive	progresivo
preside	presidir	progressively	progresivamente
presidency	presidencia	prohibition	prohibición
president	presidente	proletariat	proletario
prestige	prestigio	prologue	prólogo
presume	presumir	prolong	prolongar
pretension	pretensión	promise (n.)	promesa
pretext	pretexto	promptitude	prontitud
prevail	prevalecer	pronounce	pronunciar
prevention	prevención	propaganda	propaganda
prevision	previsión	prophet	profeta
primary	primero	propitious	propicio
primitive	primitivo	proportion	proporción
princess	princesa	proposition	proposición
principal (adj.)	principal	proprietor	propietario
principle (n.)	principio	prosaic	prosaico
prism	prisma	proscribe	proscribir
prison	prisión	prose	prosa
prisoner	prisionero	prosperity	prosperidad
privation	privación	prosperous	próspero
privilege	privilegio	protection	protección
probability	probabilidad	protector	protector
probable	probable	protest (v.)	protestar
probably	probablemente	protestant	protestante
problem	problema	protestation	protestación
proceed	proceder	proverb	proverbio
procession	procesión	providence	providencia
proclaim	proclamar	province	provincia
proclamation	proclamación	provincial	provincial
procure	procurar	provision	provisión
prodigious	prodigioso	provoke	provocar
product	producto	proximity	proximidad
production	producción	prudence	prudencia
profane	profano	prudent	prudente
profession	profesión	psychology	psicología
professional	profesional	public	público
professor	profesor	publication	publicación
profound	profundo	publicity	publicidad
profoundly	profundamente	publish	publicar
program	programa	puerile	pueril

pulpit	púlpito
pulse	pulso
pupil (eye)	pupila
pure	puro
purely	puramente
purify	purificar
pyramid	pirámide
quarter	cuarto
quiet	quieto
quietude	quietud
race (n.)	raza
radiant	radiante
radiator	radiador
radical	radical
rail	rail
ranch	rancho
rancor	rencor
rapid	rápido
rapidity	rapidez
rare	raro
rarely	raramente
rat	rato
rational	racional
ray	rayo
reaction	reacción
realist	realista
reality	realidad
realization	realización
reason (n.)	razón
reason (v.)	razonar
reasonable	razonable
rebel	rebelde
rebellion	rebelión
receive	recibir
recently	recientemente
reception	recepción
reciprocal	recíproco
recite	recitar

recommence	recomenzar
recommend	recomendar
recommendation	recomendación
recompense (n.)	recompensa
recompense (v.)	recompensar
reconcile	reconciliar
reconstitute	reconstituir
reconstruct	reconstruir
recourse	recurso
recover	recobrar
recreation	recreación
recruit (v.)	recrutar
rectangle	rectángulo
rectify	rectificar
rectitude	rectitud
redouble	redoblar
reduce	reducir
reduction	reducción
re-election	reelección
refectory	refectorio
reference	referencia
refine	refinar
refinement	refinamiento
reflect	reflejar
reflexion	reflexión
reform (n.)	reforma
reform (v.)	reformar
refractory	refractario
refuge	refugio
regale	regalar
regime	régimen
regiment	regimiento
region	región
regular	regular
regularity	regularidad
regularly	regularmente
regulator	regulador
reign (v.)	reinar
reiterate	reiterar
rejuvenate	rejuvenecer
relate	relatar

relation	relación	respire	respirar
relative (*adv.*)	relativo	resplendent	resplandeciente
relief (sculpture)	relieve	respond	responder
religion	religión	responsibility	responsabilidad
religious	religioso	responsible	responsable
remedy	remedio	rest (remainder)	resto
remedy (*v.*)	remediar	restore	restaurar
remit	remitir	result (*n.*)	resultado
renounce	renunciar	retard	retardar
renovation	renovación	retire	retirar
repair (*v.*)	reparar	return (*v.*)	retornar
reparation	reparación	reunion	reunión
repent	arrepentirse	reunite	reunir
repose (*v.*)	reposar	revelation	revelación
repose (*n.*)	reposo	reverence	reverencia
represent	representar	revision	revisión
representation	representación	revolt (*n.*)	revuelta
representative	representante	revolt (*v.*)	revoltar
repression	represión	revolutionary	revolucionario
reproach (*n.*)	reproche	revolve	revolver
reproduce	reproducir	rhetoric	retórica
reptile	reptil	rheumatism	reumatismo
republican	republicano	rich	rico
repugnance	repugnancia	ridiculous	ridículo
reputation	reputación	rigor	rigor
require	requerir	rigorous	riguroso
resentment	resentimiento	rigorously	rigurosamente
reserve (*n.*)	reserva	rite	rito
reserve (*v.*)	reservar	rival	rival
reside	residir	robust	robusto
residence	residencia	rock	roca
resignation	resignación	romance	romance
resin	resina	romantic	romántico
resist	resistir	rose	rosa
resistance	resistencia	rotund	rotundo
resolution	resolución	route (*n.*)	ruta
respect (*v.*)	respetar	rude	rudo
respectable	respetable	ruffian	rufián
respectful	respetuoso	ruin (*n.*)	ruina
respective	respectivo	ruin (*v.*)	arruinar
respiration	respiración	ruinous	ruinoso

rupture	ruptura
rural	rural
rustic	rústico
sacrifice (*n.*)	sacrificio
sacrifice (*v.*)	sacrificar
salad	ensalada
salary	salario
salient	saliente
salmon	salmón
salute (*v.*)	saludar (greet)
salvation	salvación
salvo	salva
sanction	sanción
sanctity	santidad
sane	sano
sarcasm	sarcasmo
satanical	satánico
satire	sátira
satisfaction	satisfacción
satisfactory	satisfactorio
satisfied	satisfecho
scandal	escándalo
scandalize	escandalizar
scandalous	escandaloso
scene	escena
sceptic	escéptico
scientific	científico
scruple	escrúpulo
sculpture (*n.*)	escultura
season (*v.*)	sazonar
second	segundo
secondary	secundario
secret (*n.*)	secreto
secret (*adj.*)	secreto
secretary	secretaría
secretly	secretamente
sect	secta
section	sección
secular	secular

security	seguridad
seduce	seducir
seduction	seducción
selection	selección
senate	senado
senator	senador
sensation	sensación
sensibility	sensibilidad
sensual	sensual
sentiment	sentimiento
sentimental	sentimental
separate (*v.*)	separar
separately	separadamente
separation	separación
sepulchre	sepulcro
serene	sereno
serenity	serenidad
serious	serio
sermon	sermón
serpent	serpiente
serve	servir
service	servicio
servile	servil
session	sesión
severe	severo
severely	severamente
severity	severidad
sex	sexo
sign	signo
signification	significación
signify	significar
silence	silencio
silent	silencioso
silently	silenciosamente
silhouette	silueta
simplicity	simplicidad
simplify	simplificar
simultaneous	simultáneo
simultaneously	simultáneamente
sincere	sincero
sincerely	sinceramente

sincerity	sinceridad	stupefaction	estupefacción
singular	singular	stupid	estúpido
singularly	singularmente	stupor	estupor
sinister	siniestro	style	estilo
siren	sirena	suave	suave
situate	situar	subject (n.)	sujeto
situation	situación	sublime	sublime
sobriety	sobriedad	submarine	submarino
social	social	submerge	sumergir
socialist	socialista	subordinate (v.)	subordinar
solemn	solemne	subscribe	subscribir
solemnity	solemnidad	subsist	subsistir
solicit	solicitar	substance	substancia
solicitude	solicitud	substitute (n.)	substituto
solid	sólido	substitute (v.)	substituir
solidarity	solidaridad	substitution	substitución
solidly	sólidamente	subterranean	subterraneo
solitary	solitario	subvention	subvención
soluble	soluble	succession	sucesión
solution	solución	successive	sucesivo
somber	sombrío	successively	sucesivamente
sonorous	sonoro	successor	sucesor
sophism	sofisma	succumb	sucumbir
space	espacio	suffer	sufrir
special	especial	sufficient	suficiente
specially	especialmente	sufficiently	suficientemente
speculation	especulación	suffocate	sofocar
spiral	espiral	suggestion	sugestión
spiritual	espiritual	suicide	suicidio
splendid	espléndido	sum	suma
splendor	esplendor	superficial	superficial
spontaneous	espontáneo	superfluous	superfluo
spontaneously	espontáneamente	superhuman	sobrehumano
station	estación	superintendent	superintendente
statue	estatua	superior (adv.)	superior
statute	estatuto	superiority	superioridad
sterile	estéril	supernatural	sobrenatural
stomach	estómago	superstition	superstición
strangle	estrangular	supplementary	suplementario
strictly	estrictamente	supplicant	suplicante
structure	estructura	supply	suplir

support	soportar
supposition	suposición
suppression	supresión
supreme	supremo
surprise (n.)	sorpresa
susceptible	susceptible
suspend	suspender
suspense	suspenso
suspension	suspensión
sustain	sustentar
syllable	sílaba
symbol	símbolo
syndic	síndico
syndicate	sindicato
synthetic	sintético
system	sistema
systematic	sistemático
taciturn	taciturno
tact	tacto
tactics	táctica
talent	talento
tambour	tambor
tardy	tardo
tariff	tarifa
technique	técnica
telegram	telegrama
telegraph (n.)	telégrafo
telegraph (v.)	telegrafiar
telephone	teléfono
telescope	telescopio
temperament	temperamento
temperature	temperatura
tempest	tempestad
temple	templo
temporary	temporal
tendency	tendencia
tendon	tendón
tenebrous	tenebroso
tension	tensión

terminate	terminar
terrace	terraza
terrain	terreno
terrestrial	terrestre
terrible	terrible
terribly	terriblemente
territory	territorio
terror	terror
testament	testamento
testimony	testimonio
text	texto
theatre	teatro
theme	tema
theology	teología
theoretically	teóricamente
theory	teoría
thermometer	termómetro
thesis	tesis
throne	trono
tiger	tigre
timidity	timidez
timidly	tímidamente
tint	tinte
tobacco	tabaco
tolerance	tolerancia
tolerate	tolerar
tone	tono
torment (n.)	tormento
torment (v.)	tormentar
torrent	torrente
torture (n.)	tortura
torture (v.)	torturar
totality	totalidad
totally	totalmente
tourist	turista
tradition	tradición
traditional	tradicional
tragedy	tragedia
tragic	trágico
train	tren
tranquil	tranquilo

tranquilly	tranquilamente	unity	unidad
transcendental	transcendental	universal	universal
transform	transformar	universe	universo
transformation	transformación	university (n.)	universidad
transition	transición	university (adj.)	universitario
transmit	transmitir	unjust	injusto
transparent	transparente	unstable	instable
transport (n.)	transporte	urbane	urbano
tremulous	trémulo	urgency	urgencia
trespass	traspasar	urgent	urgente
triangle	triángulo	use (v.)	usar
tribe	tribu	usual	usual
tribunal	tribunal	usurp	usurpar
tribune	tribuna	usury	usura
tricolored	tricolor	utility	utilidad
triple	triple	utilization	utilización
triumph (n.)	triunfo	utilize	utilizar
triumph (v.)	triunfar		
triumphant	triunfante	vacant	vacante
trophy	trofeo	vacation	vacaciones
tropic	trópico	vacillate	vacilar
trot	trotar	vacillation	vacilación
troubador	trovador	vagabond	vagabundo
trumpeter	trompetero	vague	vago
trunk	tronco	vaguely	vagamente
tube	tubo	valorous	valeroso
tumult	tumulto	valiant	valiente
tunic	túnica	valor	valor
tunnel	túnel	vanguard	vanguardia
turbulent	turbulento	vanity	vanidad
type	tipo	vapor	vapor
typical	típico	variable	variable
tyranny	tiranía	variation	variación
		variety	variedad
ulterior	ulterior	vary	variar
ultimate	último	vassal	vasallo
unanimous	unánime	vast	vasto
unguent (n.)	ungüento	vegetable (adj.)	vegetal
uniform (adj.)	uniforme	vehemence	vehemencia
union	unión	vehicle	vehículo
united	unido	vein	vena

velocity	velocidad	violet	violeta
vendor	vendedor	violin	violín
venerable	venerable	virgin	virgen
venerate	venerar	virile	viril
veneration	veneración	virility	virilidad
vengeance	venganza	virtue	virtud
venom	veneno	virtuous	virtuoso
venomous	venenoso	viscount	vizconde
verb	verbo	visible	visible
verbal	verbal	visibly	visiblemente
verdure	verdura	vision	visión
verify	verificar	visit (n.)	visita
verse	verso	visit (v.)	visitar
version	versión	visitor	visitador
vertical	vertical	vital	vital
veteran	veterano	vituperation	vituperio
vibrate	vibrar	vivacity	vivacidad
vice	vicio	vocation	vocación
vicious	vicioso	volcano	volcán
victim	víctima	volt	voltio
victory	victoria	volume	volumen
vigil	vigilia	voluntarily	voluntariamente
vigilance	vigilancia	voluntary	voluntario
vigor	vigor	voluptuous	voluptuoso
vigorous	vigoroso	vomit	vomitar
villain	villano	vote (n.)	voto
vinegar	vinagre	vote (v.)	votar
violation	violación	vulgar	vulgar
violence	violencia		
violent	violento		
violently	violentemente	zone	zona

A Glossary of Grammatical Terms

E. F. BLEILER

This section is intended to refresh your memory of grammatical terms or to clear up difficulties you may have had in understanding them. Before you work through the grammar, you should have a reasonably clear idea what the parts of speech and parts of a sentence are. This is not for reasons of pedantry, but simply because it is easier to talk about grammar if we agree upon terms. Grammatical terminology is as necessary to the study of grammar as the names of automobile parts are to garagemen.

This list is not exhaustive, and the definitions do not pretend to be complete, or to settle points of interpretation that grammarians have been disputing for the past several hundred years. It is a working analysis rather than a scholarly investigation. The definitions given, however, represent most typical American usage, and should serve for basic use.

The Parts of Speech

English words can be divided into eight important groups: nouns, adjectives, articles, verbs, adverbs, pronouns, prepositions, and conjunctions. The boundaries between one group of words and another are sometimes vague and ill-felt in English, but a good dictionary, like the Webster Collegiate, can help you make decisions in questionable cases. Always bear in mind, however, that the way a word is used in a sentence may be just as important as the nature of the word itself in deciding what part of speech the word is.

Nouns. *Nouns* are the *words* for *things* of all *sorts*, whether these *things* are real *objects* that you can see, or *ideas*, or *places*, or *qualities*, or *groups*, or more abstract *things*. *Examples* of *words* that are *nouns* are *cat*, *vase*, *door*, *shrub*, *wheat*, *university*, *mercy*, *intelligence*, *ocean*, *plumber*, *pleasure*, *society*, *army*. If you are in *doubt* whether a given *word* is a *noun*, try putting the *word* "my", or "this", or "large" (or some other known *adjective*) in *front* of it. If it makes *sense* in the *sentence* the *chances* are that the *word* in *question* is a *noun*. [All the *words* in *italics* in this *paragraph* are *nouns*.]

Adjectives. Adjectives are the words which delimit or give you *specific* information about the *various* nouns in a sentence. They tell you size, color, weight, pleasantness, and many *other* qualities. *Such* words as *big, expensive, terrible, insipid, hot, delightful, ruddy, informative* are all *clear* adjectives. If you are in *any* doubt whether a *certain* word is an adjective, add -er to it, or put the word "more" or "too" in front of it. If it makes *good* sense in the sentence, and does not end in -ly, the chances are that it is an adjective. (Pronoun-adjectives will be described under pronouns.) [The adjectives in the *above* sentences are in italics.]

Articles. There are only two kinds of articles in English, and they are easy to remember. The definite article is "the" and the indefinite article is "a" or "an."

Verbs. Verbs *are* the words that *tell* what action, or condition, or relationship *is going* on. Such words as *was, is, jumps, achieved, keeps, buys, sells, has finished, run, will have, may, should pay, indicates* are all verb forms. *Observe* that a verb *can be composed* of more than one word, as *will have* and *should pay*, above; these *are called* compound verbs. As a rough guide for verbs, *try adding* -ed to the word you *are wondering* about, or *taking* off an -ed that *is* already there. If it *makes* sense, the chances *are* that it *is* a verb. (This *does* not always *work*, since the so-called strong or irregular verbs *make* forms by *changing* their middle vowels, like *spring, sprang, sprung*.) [Verbs in this paragraph *are* in italics.]

Adverbs. An adverb is a word that supplies additional information about a verb, an adjective, or another adverb. It *usually* indicates time, or manner, or place, or degree. It tells you *how*, or *when*, or *where*, or to what degree things are happening. Such words as *now, then, there, not, anywhere, never, somehow, always very*, and most words ending in -ly are *ordinarily* adverbs. [Italicized words are adverbs.]

Pronouns. Pronouns are related to nouns, and take their place. (Some grammars and dictionaries group pronouns and nouns together as substantives.) They mention persons, or objects of any sort without actually giving their names.

There are several different kinds of pronouns. (1) Personal pronouns: by a grammatical convention *I, we, me, mine, us, ours* are called first person pronouns, since *they* refer to the speaker; *you* and *yours* are called second person pronouns, since *they* refer to the person addressed; and *he, him, his, she, her, hers, they, them, theirs* are called third person pronouns since *they* refer to the things or persons discussed. (2) Demonstrative pronouns: *this, that, these, those.* (3) Interrogative, or question, pronouns: *who, whom, what, whose, which.* (4) Relative pronouns, or pronouns *which* refer back to something already mentioned: *who, whom, that, which.* (5) Others: *some, any, anyone, no one, other, whichever, none*, etc.

Pronouns are difficult for *us*, since our categories are not as clear as in some other languages, and *we* use the same words for *what* foreign-language speakers see as different situations. First, our interrogative and relative pronouns overlap, and must be separated in translation. The easiest way is to observe whether a question is involved in the sentence. Examples: "*Which* [int.] do *you* like?" "The inn, *which* [rel.] was not far from Cadiz, had a restaurant." "*Who* [int.] is there?" "*I* don't know *who* [int.] was there." "The porter *who* [rel.] took our bags was Number 2132." *This* may seem to be a trivial difference to an English speaker, but in some languages *it* is very important.

Secondly, there is an overlap between pronouns and adjectives. In some cases the word "this," for example, is a pronoun; in other cases *it* is an adjective. *This* also holds true for *his, its, her, any, none, other, some, that, these, those,* and many other words. Note whether the word in question stands alone or is associated with another word. Examples: "*This* [pronoun] is mine." "This [adj.] taxi has no springs." Watch out for the word "that", which can be a pronoun or an adjective or a conjunction. And remember that "my", "your", "our", and "their" are always adjectives. [All pronouns in this section are in italics.]

Prepositions. Prepositions are the little words that introduce phrases that tell *about* condition, time, place, manner, association, degree, and similar topics. Such words as *with, in, beside, under, of, to, about, for,* and *upon* are prepositions. In English prepositions and adverbs overlap, but, as you will see *by* checking *in* your dictionary, there are usually differences *of* meaning *between* the two uses. [Prepositions *in* this paragraph are designated *by* italics.]

Conjunctions. Conjunctions are joining-words. They enable you to link words *or* groups of words into larger units, *and* to build compound *or* complex sentences out of simple sentence units. Such words as *and, but, although, or, unless,* are typical conjunctions. *Although* most conjunctions are easy enough to identify, the word "that" should be watched closely to see *that* it is not a pronoun *or* an adjective. [Conjunctions italicized.]

Words about Verbs

Verbs are responsible for most of the terminology in this short grammar. The basic terms are:

Conjugation. In many languages verbs fall into natural groups, according to the way they make their forms. These groupings are called conjugations, and are an aid to learning grammatical structure. Though it may seem difficult at first to speak of First and Second Conjugations, these are simply short ways of saying that verbs belonging to these classes make their forms according to certain consistent rules, which you can memorize.

Infinitive. This is the basic form which most dictionaries give for verbs in most languages, and in most languages it serves as the basis for classifying verbs. In English (with a very few exceptions) it has no special form. To find the infinitive for any English verb, just fill in this sentence: "I like to .... (walk, run, jump, swim, carry, disappear, etc."). The infinitive in English is usually preceded by the word "to."

Tense. This is simply a formal way of saying "time". In English we think of time as being broken into three great segments: past, present, and future. Our verbs are assigned forms to indicate this division, and are further subdivided for shades of meaning. We subdivide the present time into the present (**I walk**) and present progressive (I am walking); the past into the simple past (I walked), progressive past (I was walking), perfect or present perfect (I have walked), past perfect or pluperfect (I had walked); and future into simple future (I shall walk) and future progressive (I shall be walking). These are the most common English tenses.

Present Participles, Progressive Tenses.   In English the present participle always ends in -ing.   It can be used as a .noun or an adjective in some situations, but its chief use is in *forming* the so-called progressive tenses.   These are made by *putting* appropriate forms of the verb "to be" before a present participle: In "to walk" [an infinitive], for example, the present progressive would be: I am *walking*, you are *walking*, he is *walking*, etc.; past progressive, I was *walking*, you were *walking*, and so on.   [Present participles are in italics.]

Past Participles, Perfect Tenses.   The past participle in English is not *formed* as regularly as is the present participle.   Sometimes it is *constructed* by adding -ed or -d to the present tense, as *walked, jumped, looked, received*; but there are many verbs where it is *formed* less regularly: *seen, been, swum, chosen, brought.*   To find it, simply fill out the sentence "I have ...." putting in the verb form that your ear tells you is right for the particular verb.   If you speak grammatically, you will have the past participle.

Past participles are sometimes used as adjectives: "Don't cry over *spilt* milk."   Their most important use, however, is to form the system of verb tenses that are *called* the perfect tenses: present perfect (or perfect), past perfect (or pluperfect), etc. In English the present perfect tense is *formed* with the present tense of "to have" and the past participle of a verb: I have *walked*, you have *run*, he has *begun*, etc. The past perfect is *formed*, similarly, with the past tense of "to have" and the past participle: I had *walked*, you had *run*, he had *begun*. Most of the languages you are likely to study have similar systems of perfect tenses, though they may not be *formed* in exactly the same way as in English. [Past participles in italics.]

Preterit, Imperfect. Many languages have more than one verb tense for expressing an action that took place in the past. They may use a perfect tense (which we have just covered), or a preterit, or an imperfect. English, although you may never have thought about it, is one of these languages, for we can say "I have spoken to him" [present perfect], or "I spoke to him" [simple past], or "I was speaking to him" [past progressive]. These sentences do not mean exactly the same thing, although the differences are subtle, and are difficult to put into other words.

While usage differs a little from language to language, if a language has both a preterit and an imperfect, in general the preterit corresponds to the English simple past (I ran, I swam, I spoke), and the imperfect corresponds to the English past progressive (I was running, I was swimming, I was speaking). If you are curious to discover the mode of thought behind these different tenses, try looking at the situation in terms of background-action and point-action. One of the most important uses of the imperfect is to provide a background against which a single point-action can take place. For example, "When I was walking down the street [background, continued over a period of time, hence past progressive or imperfect], I stubbed my toe [an instant or point of time, hence a simple past or preterit]."

Reflexive. This term, which sounds more difficult than it really is, simply means that the verb flexes back upon the noun or pronoun that is its subject. In modern English the reflexive pronoun always has -self on its end, and we do not use the construction very frequently. In other languages, however, reflexive forms may be used more frequently, and in ways that do not seem very logical to an English speaker. Examples of English reflexive sentences: "He washes himself." "He seated himself at the table."

Passive. In some languages, like Latin, there is a strong feeling that an action or thing that is taking place can be expressed in two different ways. One can say, A does-something-to B, which is "active;" or B is-having-something-done-to-him by A, which is "passive." We do not have a strong feeling for this classification of experience in English, but the following examples should indicate the difference between an active and a passive verb: Active: "John is building a house." Passive: "A house is being built by John." Active: "The steamer carried the cotton to England." Passive: "The cotton was carried by the steamer to England." Bear in mind that the formation of passive verbs and the situations where they can be used vary enormously from language to language. This is one situation where you usually cannot translate English word for word into another language and make sense.

Miscellaneous Terms

Comparative, Superlative. These two terms are used with adjectives and adverbs. They indicate the degree of strength within the meaning of the word. Faster, better, earlier, newer, more rapid, more detailed, more suitable are examples of the comparative in adjectives, while more rapidly, more recently, more suitably are comparatives for adverbs. In most cases, as you have seen, the comparative uses -er or "more" for an adjective, and "more" for an adverb. Superlatives are those forms which end in -est or have "most" prefixed before them for adjectives, and "most" prefixed for adverbs: most intelligent, earliest, most rapidly, most suitably.

Gender. Gender should not be confused with actual sex. In many languages nouns are arbitrarily assigned a gender (masculine or feminine, or masculine or feminine or neuter), and this need not correspond to sex. You simply have to learn the pattern of the language you are studying in order to become familiar with its use of gender.

Idiom. An idiom is an expression that is peculiar to a language, the meaning of which is not the same as the literal meaning of the individual words composing it. Idioms, as a rule, cannot be translated word by word into another language. Examples of English idioms: "*Take it easy.*" "Don't *beat around the bush.*" "It *turned out* to be *a Dutch treat.*" "Can you *tell time* in Spanish?"

The Parts of the Sentence

Subject, Predicate. In grammar *every complete sentence* contains two basic parts, the subject and the predicate. *The subject,* if *we* state the terms most simply, is the thing, person, or activity talked about. *It* can be a noun, a pronoun, or something *that* serves as a noun. *A subject* would include, in a typical case, a noun, the articles or adjectives *which* are associated with it, and perhaps phrases. Note that in complex sentences, *each part* may have its own subject. [*The subjects of the sentences above* have been italicized.]

The predicate *talks about the subject.* In a formal sentence the predicate *includes a verb, its adverbs, predicate adjectives, phrases, and objects*—whatever *happens to be present.* A predicate adjective *is an adjective* which *happens to be in the predicate after a form of the verb to be.* Example: "Apples *are red.*" [Predicates *are in Italics.*]

In the following simple sentences subjects are in italics, predicates in italics and underlined. "*Green apples are bad for your digestion.*" "When *I go to Spain, I always stop in Cadiz.*" "*The man with the handbag is travelling to Madrid.*"

Direct and Indirect Objects. Some verbs (called transitive verbs) take direct and/or indirect objects in their predicates; other verbs (called intransitive verbs) do not take objects of any sort. In English, except for pronouns, objects do not have any special forms, but in languages which have case forms or more pronoun forms than English, objects can be troublesome.

The direct object is the person, thing, quality, or matter that the verb directs *its action* upon. It can be a pronoun, or a noun, perhaps accompanied by an article and/or adjectives. The direct object always directly follows *its verb*, except when there is also an indirect object pronoun present, which comes between the verb and the object. Prepositions do not go before direct objects. Examples: "The cook threw *green onions* into the stew." "The border guards will want to see *your passport* tomorrow." "Give *it* to me." "Please give me *a glass of red wine.*" [We have placed *direct objects* in this paragraph in italics.]

The indirect object, as grammars will tell *you*, is the person or thing for or to whom the action is taking place. It can be a pronoun or a noun with or without article and adjectives. In most cases the words "to" or "for" can be inserted before it, if not already there. Examples: "Please tell *me* the time." "I wrote *her* a letter from Barcelona." "We sent *Mr. Gonzalez* ten pesos." "We gave *the most energetic guide* a large tip." [Indirect objects are in italics.]

INDEX

The following abbreviations have been used in this index; *adj.* for adjective, *conj.* for conjugation, *def.* for definition, *prep.* for preposition, *pron.* for pronoun and *vb.* for verb. Spanish words appear in *italics* and their English translations in parentheses.

A CATALOG OF SELECTED
DOVER BOOKS
IN ALL FIELDS OF INTEREST

A CATALOG OF SELECTED DOVER
BOOKS IN ALL FIELDS OF INTEREST

CONCERNING THE SPIRITUAL IN ART, Wassily Kandinsky. Pioneering work by father of abstract art. Thoughts on color theory, nature of art. Analysis of earlier masters. 12 illustrations. 80pp. of text. 5⅜ × 8½. 23411-8 Pa. $3.95

ANIMALS: 1,419 Copyright-Free Illustrations of Mammals, Birds, Fish, Insects, etc., Jim Harter (ed.). Clear wood engravings present, in extremely lifelike poses, over 1,000 species of animals. One of the most extensive pictorial sourcebooks of its kind. Captions. Index. 284pp. 9 × 12. 23766-4 Pa. $12.95

CELTIC ART: The Methods of Construction, George Bain. Simple geometric techniques for making Celtic interlacements, spirals, Kells-type initials, animals, humans, etc. Over 500 illustrations. 160pp. 9 × 12. (USO) 22923-8 Pa. $9.95

AN ATLAS OF ANATOMY FOR ARTISTS, Fritz Schider. Most thorough reference work on art anatomy in the world. Hundreds of illustrations, including selections from works by Vesalius, Leonardo, Goya, Ingres, Michelangelo, others. 593 illustrations. 192pp. 7⅛ × 10¼. 20241-0 Pa. $9.95

CELTIC HAND STROKE-BY-STROKE (Irish Half-Uncial from "The Book of Kells"): An Arthur Baker Calligraphy Manual, Arthur Baker. Complete guide to creating each letter of the alphabet in distinctive Celtic manner. Covers hand position, strokes, pens, inks, paper, more. Illustrated. 48pp. 8¼ × 11. 24336-2 Pa. $3.95

EASY ORIGAMI, John Montroll. Charming collection of 32 projects (hat, cup, pelican, piano, swan, many more) specially designed for the novice origami hobbyist. Clearly illustrated easy-to-follow instructions insure that even beginning papercrafters will achieve successful results. 48pp. 8¼ × 11. 27298-2 Pa. $2.95

THE COMPLETE BOOK OF BIRDHOUSE CONSTRUCTION FOR WOOD-WORKERS, Scott D. Campbell. Detailed instructions, illustrations, tables. Also data on bird habitat and instinct patterns. Bibliography. 3 tables. 63 illustrations in 15 figures. 48pp. 5¼ × 8½. 24407-5 Pa. $1.95

BLOOMINGDALE'S ILLUSTRATED 1886 CATALOG: Fashions, Dry Goods and Housewares, Bloomingdale Brothers. Famed merchants' extremely rare catalog depicting about 1,700 products: clothing, housewares, firearms, dry goods, jewelry, more. Invaluable for dating, identifying vintage items. Also, copyright-free graphics for artists, designers. Co-published with Henry Ford Museum & Greenfield Village. 160pp. 8¼ × 11. 25780-0 Pa. $9.95

HISTORIC COSTUME IN PICTURES, Braun & Schneider. Over 1,450 costumed figures in clearly detailed engravings—from dawn of civilization to end of 19th century. Captions. Many folk costumes. 256pp. 8⅜ × 11¾. 23150-X Pa. $11.95

EARLY NINETEENTH-CENTURY CRAFTS AND TRADES, Peter Stockham (ed.). Extremely rare 1807 volume describes to youngsters the crafts and trades of the day: brickmaker, weaver, dressmaker, bookbinder, ropemaker, saddler, many more. Quaint prose, charming illustrations for each craft. 20 black-and-white line illustrations. 192pp. 4⅝ × 6. 27293-1 Pa. $4.95

VICTORIAN FASHIONS AND COSTUMES FROM HARPER'S BAZAR, 1867–1898, Stella Blum (ed.). Day costumes, evening wear, sports clothes, shoes, hats, other accessories in over 1,000 detailed engravings. 320pp. 9⅜ × 12¼.
22990-4 Pa. $13.95

GUSTAV STICKLEY, THE CRAFTSMAN, Mary Ann Smith. Superb study surveys broad scope of Stickley's achievement, especially in architecture. Design philosophy, rise and fall of the Craftsman empire, descriptions and floor plans for many Craftsman houses, more. 86 black-and-white halftones. 31 line illustrations. Introduction. 208pp. 6½ × 9¼. 27210-9 Pa. $9.95

THE LONG ISLAND RAIL ROAD IN EARLY PHOTOGRAPHS, Ron Ziel. Over 220 rare photos, informative text document origin (1844) and development of rail service on Long Island. Vintage views of early trains, locomotives, stations, passengers, crews, much more. Captions. 8⅞ × 11¾. 26301-0 Pa. $13.95

THE BOOK OF OLD SHIPS: From Egyptian Galleys to Clipper Ships, Henry B. Culver. Superb, authoritative history of sailing vessels, with 80 magnificent line illustrations. Galley, bark, caravel, longship, whaler, many more. Detailed, informative text on each vessel by noted naval historian. Introduction. 256pp. 5⅜ × 8½. 27332-6 Pa. $6.95

TEN BOOKS ON ARCHITECTURE, Vitruvius. The most important book ever written on architecture. Early Roman aesthetics, technology, classical orders, site selection, all other aspects. Morgan translation. 331pp. 5⅜ × 8½. 20645-9 Pa. $8.95

THE HUMAN FIGURE IN MOTION, Eadweard Muybridge. More than 4,500 stopped-action photos, in action series, showing undraped men, women, children jumping, lying down, throwing, sitting, wrestling, carrying, etc. 390pp. 7⅞ × 10⅝.
20204-6 Clothbd. $24.95

TREES OF THE EASTERN AND CENTRAL UNITED STATES AND CANADA, William M. Harlow. Best one-volume guide to 140 trees. Full descriptions, woodlore, range, etc. Over 600 illustrations. Handy size. 288pp. 4½ × 6⅜.
20395-6 Pa. $5.95

SONGS OF WESTERN BIRDS, Dr. Donald J. Borror. Complete song and call repertoire of 60 western species, including flycatchers, juncoes, cactus wrens, many more—includes fully illustrated booklet. Cassette and manual 99913-0 $8.95

GROWING AND USING HERBS AND SPICES, Milo Miloradovich. Versatile handbook provides all the information needed for cultivation and use of all the herbs and spices available in North America. 4 illustrations. Index. Glossary. 236pp. 5⅜ × 8½. 25058-X Pa. $6.95

BIG BOOK OF MAZES AND LABYRINTHS, Walter Shepherd. 50 mazes and labyrinths in all—classical, solid, ripple, and more—in one great volume. Perfect inexpensive puzzler for clever youngsters. Full solutions. 112pp. 8⅛ × 11.
22951-3 Pa. $4.95

CATALOG OF DOVER BOOKS

PIANO TUNING, J. Cree Fischer. Clearest, best book for beginner, amateur. Simple repairs, raising dropped notes, tuning by easy method of flattened fifths. No previous skills needed. 4 illustrations. 201pp. 5⅜ × 8½. 23267-0 Pa. $5.95

A SOURCE BOOK IN THEATRICAL HISTORY, A. M. Nagler. Contemporary observers on acting, directing, make-up, costuming, stage props, machinery, scene design, from Ancient Greece to Chekhov. 611pp. 5⅜ × 8½. 20515-0 Pa. $11.95

THE COMPLETE NONSENSE OF EDWARD LEAR, Edward Lear. All nonsense limericks, zany alphabets, Owl and Pussycat, songs, nonsense botany, etc., illustrated by Lear. Total of 320pp. 5⅜ × 8½. (USO) 20167-8 Pa. $6.95

VICTORIAN PARLOUR POETRY: An Annotated Anthology, Michael R. Turner. 117 gems by Longfellow, Tennyson, Browning, many lesser-known poets. "The Village Blacksmith," "Curfew Must Not Ring Tonight," "Only a Baby Small," dozens more, often difficult to find elsewhere. Index of poets, titles, first lines. xxiii + 325pp. 5⅜ × 8¼. 27044-0 Pa. $8.95

DUBLINERS, James Joyce. Fifteen stories offer vivid, tightly focused observations of the lives of Dublin's poorer classes. At least one, "The Dead," is considered a masterpiece. Reprinted complete and unabridged from standard edition. 160pp. 5³/₁₆ × 8¼. 26870-5 Pa. $1.00

THE HAUNTED MONASTERY and THE CHINESE MAZE MURDERS, Robert van Gulik. Two full novels by van Gulik, set in 7th-century China, continue adventures of Judge Dee and his companions. An evil Taoist monastery, seemingly supernatural events; overgrown topiary maze hides strange crimes. 27 illustrations. 328pp. 5⅜ × 8½. 23502-5 Pa. $7.95

THE BOOK OF THE SACRED MAGIC OF ABRAMELIN THE MAGE, translated by S. MacGregor Mathers. Medieval manuscript of ceremonial magic. Basic document in Aleister Crowley, Golden Dawn groups. 268pp. 5⅜ × 8½. 23211-5 Pa. $8.95

NEW RUSSIAN-ENGLISH AND ENGLISH-RUSSIAN DICTIONARY, M. A. O'Brien. This is a remarkably handy Russian dictionary, containing a surprising amount of information, including over 70,000 entries. 366pp. 4½ × 6⅛. 20208-9 Pa. $9.95

HISTORIC HOMES OF THE AMERICAN PRESIDENTS, Second, Revised Edition, Irvin Haas. A traveler's guide to American Presidential homes, most open to the public, depicting and describing homes occupied by every American President from George Washington to George Bush. With visiting hours, admission charges, travel routes. 175 photographs. Index. 160pp. 8¼ × 11. 26751-2 Pa. $10.95

NEW YORK IN THE FORTIES, Andreas Feininger. 162 brilliant photographs by the well-known photographer, formerly with *Life* magazine. Commuters, shoppers, Times Square at night, much else from city at its peak. Captions by John von Hartz. 181pp. 9¼ × 10¾. 23585-8 Pa. $12.95

INDIAN SIGN LANGUAGE, William Tomkins. Over 525 signs developed by Sioux and other tribes. Written instructions and diagrams. Also 290 pictographs. 111pp. 6⅛ × 9¼. 22029-X Pa. $3.50

ANATOMY: A Complete Guide for Artists, Joseph Sheppard. A master of figure drawing shows artists how to render human anatomy convincingly. Over 460 illustrations. 224pp. 8⅜ × 11¼. 27279-6 Pa. $10.95

MEDIEVAL CALLIGRAPHY: Its History and Technique, Marc Drogin. Spirited history, comprehensive instruction manual covers 13 styles (ca. 4th century thru 15th). Excellent photographs; directions for duplicating medieval techniques with modern tools. 224pp. 8⅜ × 11¼. 26142-5 Pa. $11.95

DRIED FLOWERS: How to Prepare Them, Sarah Whitlock and Martha Rankin. Complete instructions on how to use silica gel, meal and borax, perlite aggregate, sand and borax, glycerine and water to create attractive permanent flower arrangements. 12 illustrations. 32pp. 5⅜ × 8½. 21802-3 Pa. $1.00

EASY-TO-MAKE BIRD FEEDERS FOR WOODWORKERS, Scott D. Campbell. Detailed, simple-to-use guide for designing, constructing, caring for and using feeders. Text, illustrations for 12 classic and contemporary designs. 96pp. 5⅜ × 8½. 25847-5 Pa. $2.95

OLD-TIME CRAFTS AND TRADES, Peter Stockham. An 1807 book created to teach children about crafts and trades open to them as future careers. It describes in detailed, nontechnical terms 24 different occupations, among them coachmaker, gardener, hairdresser, lacemaker, shoemaker, wheelwright, copper-plate printer, milliner, trunkmaker, merchant and brewer. Finely detailed engravings illustrate each occupation. 192pp. 4⅝ × 6. 27398-9 Pa. $4.95

THE HISTORY OF UNDERCLOTHES, C. Willett Cunnington and Phyllis Cunnington. Fascinating, well-documented survey covering six centuries of English undergarments, enhanced with over 100 illustrations: 12th-century laced-up bodice, footed long drawers (1795), 19th-century bustles, 19th-century corsets for men, Victorian "bust improvers," much more. 272pp. 5⅜ × 8¼. 27124-2 Pa. $9.95

ARTS AND CRAFTS FURNITURE: The Complete Brooks Catalog of 1912, Brooks Manufacturing Co. Photos and detailed descriptions of more than 150 now very collectible furniture designs from the Arts and Crafts movement depict davenports, settees, buffets, desks, tables, chairs, bedsteads, dressers and more, all built of solid, quarter-sawed oak. Invaluable for students and enthusiasts of antiques, Americana and the decorative arts. 80pp. 6½ × 9¼. 27471-3 Pa. $7.95

HOW WE INVENTED THE AIRPLANE: An Illustrated History, Orville Wright. Fascinating firsthand account covers early experiments, construction of planes and motors, first flights, much more. Introduction and commentary by Fred C. Kelly. 76 photographs. 96pp. 8¼ × 11. 25662-6 Pa. $8.95

THE ARTS OF THE SAILOR: Knotting, Splicing and Ropework, Hervey Garrett Smith. Indispensable shipboard reference covers tools, basic knots and useful hitches; handsewing and canvas work, more. Over 100 illustrations. Delightful reading for sea lovers. 256pp. 5⅜ × 8½. 26440-8 Pa. $7.95

FRANK LLOYD WRIGHT'S FALLINGWATER: The House and Its History, Second, Revised Edition, Donald Hoffmann. A total revision—both in text and illustrations—of the standard document on Fallingwater, the boldest, most personal architectural statement of Wright's mature years, updated with valuable new material from the recently opened Frank Lloyd Wright Archives. "Fascinating"—*The New York Times.* 116 illustrations. 128pp. 9¼ × 10¾. 27430-6 Pa. $10.95

PHOTOGRAPHIC SKETCHBOOK OF THE CIVIL WAR, Alexander Gardner. 100 photos taken on field during the Civil War. Famous shots of Manassas, Harper's Ferry, Lincoln, Richmond, slave pens, etc. 244pp. 10⅝ × 8¼.
22731-6 Pa. $9.95

FIVE ACRES AND INDEPENDENCE, Maurice G. Kains. Great back-to-the-land classic explains basics of self-sufficient farming. The one book to get. 95 illustrations. 397pp. 5⅜ × 8½.
20974-1 Pa. $7.95

SONGS OF EASTERN BIRDS, Dr. Donald J. Borror. Songs and calls of 60 species most common to eastern U.S.: warblers, woodpeckers, flycatchers, thrushes, larks, many more in high-quality recording.
Cassette and manual 99912-2 $8.95

A MODERN HERBAL, Margaret Grieve. Much the fullest, most exact, most useful compilation of herbal material. Gigantic alphabetical encyclopedia, from aconite to zedoary, gives botanical information, medical properties, folklore, economic uses, much else. Indispensable to serious reader. 161 illustrations. 888pp. 6½ × 9¼. 2-vol. set. (USO)
Vol. I: 22798-7 Pa. $9.95
Vol. II: 22799-5 Pa. $9.95

HIDDEN TREASURE MAZE BOOK, Dave Phillips. Solve 34 challenging mazes accompanied by heroic tales of adventure. Evil dragons, people-eating plants, bloodthirsty giants, many more dangerous adversaries lurk at every twist and turn. 34 mazes, stories, solutions. 48pp. 8¼ × 11.
24566-7 Pa. $2.95

LETTERS OF W. A. MOZART, Wolfgang A. Mozart. Remarkable letters show bawdy wit, humor, imagination, musical insights, contemporary musical world; includes some letters from Leopold Mozart. 276pp. 5⅜ × 8½.
22859-2 Pa. $7.95

BASIC PRINCIPLES OF CLASSICAL BALLET, Agrippina Vaganova. Great Russian theoretician, teacher explains methods for teaching classical ballet. 118 illustrations. 175pp. 5⅜ × 8½.
22036-2 Pa. $4.95

THE JUMPING FROG, Mark Twain. Revenge edition. The original story of The Celebrated Jumping Frog of Calaveras County, a hapless French translation, and Twain's hilarious "retranslation" from the French. 12 illustrations. 66pp. 5⅜ × 8½.
22686-7 Pa. $3.95

BEST REMEMBERED POEMS, Martin Gardner (ed.). The 126 poems in this superb collection of 19th- and 20th-century British and American verse range from Shelley's "To a Skylark" to the impassioned "Renascence" of Edna St. Vincent Millay and to Edward Lear's whimsical "The Owl and the Pussycat." 224pp. 5⅜ × 8½.
27165-X Pa. $4.95

COMPLETE SONNETS, William Shakespeare. Over 150 exquisite poems deal with love, friendship, the tyranny of time, beauty's evanescence, death and other themes in language of remarkable power, precision and beauty. Glossary of archaic terms. 80pp. 5³/₁₆ × 8¼.
26686-9 Pa. $1.00

BODIES IN A BOOKSHOP, R. T. Campbell. Challenging mystery of blackmail and murder with ingenious plot and superbly drawn characters. In the best tradition of British suspense fiction. 192pp. 5⅜ × 8½.
24720-1 Pa. $5.95

THE WIT AND HUMOR OF OSCAR WILDE, Alvin Redman (ed.). More than 1,000 ripostes, paradoxes, wisecracks: Work is the curse of the drinking classes; I can resist everything except temptation; etc. 258pp. 5⅜ × 8½. 20602-5 Pa. $5.95

SHAKESPEARE LEXICON AND QUOTATION DICTIONARY, Alexander Schmidt. Full definitions, locations, shades of meaning in every word in plays and poems. More than 50,000 exact quotations. 1,485pp. 6½ × 9¼. 2-vol. set.
Vol. I: 22726-X Pa. $16.95
Vol. 2: 22727-8 Pa. $15.95

SELECTED POEMS, Emily Dickinson. Over 100 best-known, best-loved poems by one of America's foremost poets, reprinted from authoritative early editions. No comparable edition at this price. Index of first lines. 64pp. 5³⁄₁₆ × 8¼.
26466-1 Pa. $1.00

CELEBRATED CASES OF JUDGE DEE (DEE GOONG AN), translated by Robert van Gulik. Authentic 18th-century Chinese detective novel; Dee and associates solve three interlocked cases. Led to van Gulik's own stories with same characters. Extensive introduction. 9 illustrations. 237pp. 5⅜ × 8½.
23337-5 Pa. $6.95

THE MALLEUS MALEFICARUM OF KRAMER AND SPRENGER, translated by Montague Summers. Full text of most important witchhunter's "bible," used by both Catholics and Protestants. 278pp. 6⅝ × 10. 22802-9 Pa. $11.95

SPANISH STORIES/CUENTOS ESPAÑOLES: A Dual-Language Book, Angel Flores (ed.). Unique format offers 13 great stories in Spanish by Cervantes, Borges, others. Faithful English translations on facing pages. 352pp. 5⅜ × 8½.
25399-6 Pa. $8.95

THE CHICAGO WORLD'S FAIR OF 1893: A Photographic Record, Stanley Appelbaum (ed.). 128 rare photos show 200 buildings, Beaux-Arts architecture, Midway, original Ferris Wheel, Edison's kinetoscope, more. Architectural emphasis; full text. 116pp. 8¼ × 11. 23990-X Pa. $9.95

OLD QUEENS, N.Y., IN EARLY PHOTOGRAPHS, Vincent F. Seyfried and William Asadorian. Over 160 rare photographs of Maspeth, Jamaica, Jackson Heights, and other areas. Vintage views of DeWitt Clinton mansion, 1939 World's Fair and more. Captions. 192pp. 8⅞ × 11. 26358-4 Pa. $12.95

CAPTURED BY THE INDIANS: 15 Firsthand Accounts, 1750–1870, Frederick Drimmer. Astounding true historical accounts of grisly torture, bloody conflicts, relentless pursuits, miraculous escapes and more, by people who lived to tell the tale. 384pp. 5⅜ × 8½. 24901-8 Pa. $8.95

THE WORLD'S GREAT SPEECHES, Lewis Copeland and Lawrence W. Lamm (eds.). Vast collection of 278 speeches of Greeks to 1970. Powerful and effective models; unique look at history. 842pp. 5⅜ × 8½. 20468-5 Pa. $14.95

THE BOOK OF THE SWORD, Sir Richard F. Burton. Great Victorian scholar/adventurer's eloquent, erudite history of the "queen of weapons"—from prehistory to early Roman Empire. Evolution and development of early swords, variations (sabre, broadsword, cutlass, scimitar, etc.), much more. 336pp. 6⅛ × 9¼. 25434-8 Pa. $8.95

AUTOBIOGRAPHY: The Story of My Experiments with Truth, Mohandas K. Gandhi. Boyhood, legal studies, purification, the growth of the Satyagraha (nonviolent protest) movement. Critical, inspiring work of the man responsible for the freedom of India. 480pp. 5⅜ × 8½. (USO) 24593-4 Pa. $8.95

CELTIC MYTHS AND LEGENDS, T. W. Rolleston. Masterful retelling of Irish and Welsh stories and tales. Cuchulain, King Arthur, Deirdre, the Grail, many more. First paperback edition. 58 full-page illustrations. 512pp. 5⅜ × 8½. 26507-2 Pa. $9.95

THE PRINCIPLES OF PSYCHOLOGY, William James. Famous long course complete, unabridged. Stream of thought, time perception, memory, experimental methods; great work decades ahead of its time. 94 figures. 1,391pp. 5⅜ × 8½. 2-vol. set.
Vol. I: 20381-6 Pa. $12.95
Vol. II: 20382-4 Pa. $12.95

THE WORLD AS WILL AND REPRESENTATION, Arthur Schopenhauer. Definitive English translation of Schopenhauer's life work, correcting more than 1,000 errors, omissions in earlier translations. Translated by E. F. J. Payne. Total of 1,269pp. 5⅜ × 8½. 2-vol. set.
Vol. 1: 21761-2 Pa. $11.95
Vol. 2: 21762-0 Pa. $11.95

MAGIC AND MYSTERY IN TIBET, Madame Alexandra David-Neel. Experiences among lamas, magicians, sages, sorcerers, Bonpa wizards. A true psychic discovery. 32 illustrations. 321pp. 5⅜ × 8½. (USO) 22682-4 Pa. $8.95

THE EGYPTIAN BOOK OF THE DEAD, E. A. Wallis Budge. Complete reproduction of Ani's papyrus, finest ever found. Full hieroglyphic text, interlinear transliteration, word-for-word translation, smooth translation. 533pp. 6½ × 9¼. 21866-X Pa. $9.95

MATHEMATICS FOR THE NONMATHEMATICIAN, Morris Kline. Detailed, college-level treatment of mathematics in cultural and historical context, with numerous exercises. Recommended Reading Lists. Tables. Numerous figures. 641pp. 5⅜ × 8½. 24823-2 Pa. $11.95

THEORY OF WING SECTIONS: Including a Summary of Airfoil Data, Ira H. Abbott and A. E. von Doenhoff. Concise compilation of subsonic aerodynamic characteristics of NACA wing sections, plus description of theory. 350pp. of tables. 693pp. 5⅜ × 8½. 60586-8 Pa. $14.95

THE RIME OF THE ANCIENT MARINER, Gustave Doré, S. T. Coleridge. Doré's finest work; 34 plates capture moods, subtleties of poem. Flawless full-size reproductions printed on facing pages with authoritative text of poem. "Beautiful. Simply beautiful."—*Publisher's Weekly*. 77pp. 9¼ × 12. 22305-1 Pa. $6.95

NORTH AMERICAN INDIAN DESIGNS FOR ARTISTS AND CRAFTSPEOPLE, Eva Wilson. Over 360 authentic copyright-free designs adapted from Navajo blankets, Hopi pottery, Sioux buffalo hides, more. Geometrics, symbolic figures, plant and animal motifs, etc. 128pp. 8⅜ × 11. (EUK) 25341-4 Pa. $7.95

SCULPTURE: Principles and Practice, Louis Slobodkin. Step-by-step approach to clay, plaster, metals, stone; classical and modern. 253 drawings, photos. 255pp. 8⅛ × 11. 22960-2 Pa. $10.95

THE INFLUENCE OF SEA POWER UPON HISTORY, 1000–1783, A. T. Mahan. Influential classic of naval history and tactics still used as text in war colleges. First paperback edition. 4 maps. 24 battle plans. 640pp. 5⅜ × 8½.
25509-3 Pa. $12.95

THE STORY OF THE TITANIC AS TOLD BY ITS SURVIVORS, Jack Winocour (ed.). What it was really like. Panic, despair, shocking inefficiency, and a little heroism. More thrilling than any fictional account. 26 illustrations. 320pp. 5⅜ × 8½.
20610-6 Pa. $8.95

FAIRY AND FOLK TALES OF THE IRISH PEASANTRY, William Butler Yeats (ed.). Treasury of 64 tales from the twilight world of Celtic myth and legend: "The Soul Cages," "The Kildare Pooka," "King O'Toole and his Goose," many more. Introduction and Notes by W. B. Yeats. 352pp. 5⅜ × 8½.
26941-8 Pa. $8.95

BUDDHIST MAHAYANA TEXTS, E. B. Cowell and Others (eds.). Superb, accurate translations of basic documents in Mahayana Buddhism, highly important in history of religions. The Buddha-karita of Asvaghosha, Larger Sukhavativyuha, more. 448pp. 5⅜ × 8½. ,
25552-2 Pa. $9.95

ONE TWO THREE . . . INFINITY: Facts and Speculations of Science, George Gamow. Great physicist's fascinating, readable overview of contemporary science: number theory, relativity, fourth dimension, entropy, genes, atomic structure, much more. 128 illustrations. Index. 352pp. 5⅜ × 8½.
25664-2 Pa. $8.95

ENGINEERING IN HISTORY, Richard Shelton Kirby, et al. Broad, nontechnical survey of history's major technological advances: birth of Greek science, industrial revolution, electricity and applied science, 20th-century automation, much more. 181 illustrations. ". . . excellent . . ."—Isis. Bibliography. vii + 530pp. 5⅜ × 8¼.
26412-2 Pa. $14.95